Root River Return

Root River Return

A MEMOIR

BY DAVID KHERDIAN

Beech Hill Publishing Company
Mount Desert, Maine

BEECH HILL PUBLISHING COMPANY
Mount Desert, Maine 04660

© 2015 by David Kherdian

ISBN: 978-0-9908200-2-4

Printed on acid-free paper in the United States of America

Cover art by Nonny Hogrogian

www.beechhillpublishingcompany.com

For Nonny

Contents

I

Prologue: Racine, 1935, 3
The First Memory of
    My Father, 6
Root River, 7
Drawing, 8
Poem, 9
Father's Furnace, 10
Father, 11
The Art of Kindergarten, 12
Irises, 13
That Day, 14
Island Park, 15
The Emperor of
    Ice Cream, 16
Mulberry Trees, 17
Father's Hands. 18
The One Day, 20
Horses, 21
The Fishermen, 22
Saturdays with Father, 25
Windows, 27
Outdoors, 28
Our Sparrows, 29
Pantries, 31
Home, 32
Remember, 33
The Coffee House, 34
The Birthday, 36
The Accident, 37
Dedeh, 38

To My Father, 40
The Nights, 42
The Pond, 43
Harry Gaykian, 44
Parks and the River, 46
Above Island Park, 47
Baseball & Father, 48
Uncle Jack, 49
In Father's Garden. 52
United States Tony, 53
Herbert Von Haden, 55

II

The Vision, 59
The Song, 60
Root River, 61
Calling My Name, 62
For Nazeli, 63
Joe Perch, 64
Foundry, 70
Father, 71
The Bins, 72
The Crab & Minnow Bait
    Garages, 73
Hovhannes Pahltahlian, 75
Chuck Pehlivanian, 77
Yo-Yos, 80
Dominic Galati, 81
Horlick's Athletic Field, 82
Poem, 84
The Hunters, 85

Lake Michigan, 86

Histories, 88

Ray Rodriguez, 89

Dear Mrs. McKinney
    of the Sixth Grade, 92

Itinerants, 94

William Miller, 96

Our Fathers, 98

Yellow Bricks, 100

Stu Faber, 101

Charles Kamakian, 103

Nancy Jacobsen, 104

Our Library, 106

Thompsondale, 107

The Runaway, 108

Below, 109

Pigeons, 110

Then, 111

The Bridge, 112

III

10 Years Later, 115

I didn't want to protect
    myself, 116

Island Park, 117

The Peasant, 118

Armenian Coffee
    Houses, 119

Willie, 120

Kewpees, 121

Friday Night Fish Fry, 123

The Trains, 124

Father's Turk, 126

Abby, 127

1950, 128

Father's America, 130

Gob Kaiserlian, 131

Father, 134

Dafje Vartan, 135

The Lake, 136

Going, 138

Father's Time, 140

Beside the River

Book One, 145

Book Two, 183

Glossary, 209

I

Prologue

"Today we are going downtown," Mother said. She was kneeling in front of me, buttoning my coat. I liked being close to her. There was a dent, like a hole almost, in the corner of her lip. I reached out and touched it with my finger.

"What's that, Mama?"

"That's my Aleppo Button."

"What's an Aleppo, Mama?"

"Aleppo is a city in the old country where the water is so bad that everyone who passes through is given a button in remembrance." Mother laughed.

"On the lip, like you?"

"No . . . in various places, but usually on the face."

"Why, Mama?"

"I was a refugee, after the Massacres, without a home or a place to stay—and then I went to the orphanage."

"Did you get the button in the orphanage?"

"Yes, darling, while I was in the orphanage."

"Tell me again about downtown, Mama."

"Downtown is where every building is a store—and then, way at the end, there is Monument Square. Water and fish and grass and flowers. Just what you like! But first we are going to the Rex Theatre to see Valentino in a movie. Your first movie! Then we'll shop, and I'll show you Monument Square."

I felt happy. When Mother finished dressing me, we walked outside. It was windy and the leaves were different colors. Some of them flew off the trees as I held Mother's hand.

We walked all the way to the corner and then we turned. "This is State Street," Mother said. "Can you see where it ends? Far,

far away. See?" "I think so," I said.

"That's the movie house."

"The Rex Theatre!" I exclaimed.

"Yes! You remembered!" Mother smiled down at me and squeezed my hand.

The first building we had seen when we turned the corner onto State Street was the church. Then we had come to a large house, followed by several stores. Some of the doors were closed, but one was open. There were men inside, talking. The whole next block was one long building. I stared up at all the windows.

"This is the J. I. Case office," Mother said. "Across the street is the factory where Papa works."

I turned my head and looked back at the big place where Papa worked. Mother gently pulled my arm.

By the time we crossed the street I had forgotten Papa. "This is Douglas Avenue," Mother said. We turned together and looked up the street. I could see the Massis Hotel when Mother pointed to it, but I couldn't see the Three Kings Tavern that Mother said was on the other side of the street. "That's where Mikey's father works, with all the other Kaiserlians," Mother said.

We had stopped. Then we began walking again. All the buildings were stuck together. "Why, Mama?" I asked.

"Taverns, mostly," Mother said and made one of her faces that I didn't like. There are men inside. When they don't work, they drink and talk loud."

I understood. They were keeping the noises inside. They had put the buildings together so the noises wouldn't leak out. "Are they Turks?" I asked.

"No," Mother said and smiled. "They are Americans."

I wanted to ask about the Americans, but I was scared. Who were the Americans? Who were the Armenians? Why were they different? I looked up at Mother, but she didn't tell me.

We walked up and up and up: all at once I couldn't see the Rex

Theatre anymore. I began to get scared, but the smoke started coming up from the ground just ahead of me. I looked down at the sidewalk and then ahead at the smoke.

"It's coming from the boats on Root River," Mother said." They're under the bridge."

I let go of Mother's hand and ran with all my might. When I got to the bridge I held onto the railing. I felt scared and excited all at once. I looked at the boat and then back at Mama. I didn't know how to say what I was seeing.

"Mama, Mama!" I kept shouting. I pointed down. Mama came and looked with me at the boat. Then I watched the big white and gray birds that followed it. The boat whistled. Behind it the water pushed up and away. The birds were making hungry calls at the boat, but the boat didn't care. It kept going and going. Maybe it couldn't stop.

The boat got smaller and smaller. The big birds were flying after it, but then one, all gray, flew over the bridge and looked at me. I was afraid to wave, and then I waved. He flew after the other birds. He belonged to the boat too.

Then everything was quiet and I felt quiet too. The smoke was gone, and the water stopped moving.

I took Mother's hand and she started to walk, but I wouldn't let go of the bridge railing. Way below were the water and the big wooden poles coming out of the water. They belonged there. But the boat was gone with the birds.

The First Memory of My Father

The earliest remembrance of my father taking me
for a walk out for a few hours perhaps on a Sunday
and we were in the park—Island Park—and someone
was in a buggy was it me no we had stopped for an
exchange was it my Uncle Jack or still another
but Uncle was surely there too and the feeling
was warm that was it a warm exchange of love
not just between them or us or us and another
the one in the carriage and the other like my father
also walking or carrying one like myself out for
a walk and the day but between everything and everyone
the sun the breeze the low green voices dissolving
in movement absorbed by the bushes and the breeze
but a feeling a feeling of love between people
and to that I have attached a life.

Root River

Drawn into inlets
by transparent minnows—
suddenly gone to myself
and following where they lead,
I fall to my knees
to catch them,
though to catch them
is not what I want;
and they lead me to
underwater grasses,
razor sharp pebbles
and silt and mud hollows
of tadpoles and star-
flecked sun-spotted falls,
into a home I can
never leave,
dreaming of fish,
breathing fish
swimming into fish

Drawing

Before anything else I wanted to draw.
At home, in the living room
with the radio on—
mother sometimes sewing,
father alone with his thoughts,
I took pencil to paper and drew,
copying landscapes from works
I admired, that put me far beyond—
near crystal streams I imagined
and silent waterfalls

Or to something so close by
that insects and crickets sprang
into the air with their busy songs,
inviting my soul to enter there—
my pencil slowly noting the way

Poem

Wandering the river
at Island Park
holding the hand
of my uncle
we spot simultaneously
for the first time
a bullhead lazily
swimming the
river's bank
unfrightened of us
and around her
miniature fry
so perfect in their
tiny completeness
that my breath
stopped for a moment
overwhelmed by
their beauty
and the love they
conveyed to my heart
and ever after
uncle was a part
of that feeling
that discovery
of what exists

between Heaven and Earth

Father's Furnace

I would hear the iron clank
and know you were shoveling
coal into the orange mouth
 of the hungry black furnace

and I would roll over in my
half-sleep, curling my body
for additional warmth

while Mother rose and readied
breakfast, calling me to dress
before the parlor vent

that brought a draft of warming air
from where you had been
before you went off, trudging

down the cold dark street
of icy wind-swept snow
in your heavy gray coat

waiting at the corner for the bus
that would take you
to the factory gate alone.

Father

I think of him trudging off
in winter snow by
morning dark
to wait
at the corner
bus stop
end of our block

And the lonely, tubular
light of the bus
traveling the deserted
streets of our town
taking those early morning
men to their jobs

And also walking home
in summer, four miles
of city streets, from the
factory gate to where
I stood on the sidewalk

Or sometimes on the porch
waiting to be greeted
as he had waited to greet
me, pressing a nickel or
dime into my palm,
still warm from his hand,
money he had saved from
the fare, that I was to use
for ice cream
or whatever else I might
want

The Art of Kindergarten

For years I kept it and then it was lost.
My first report card! But you will not
understand by that name what it was for me.
It had come on rose colored crepe paper,
long and narrow in shape, and there were
pasted-down strips, perhaps typed, but
more likely written carefully in a feminine—
and this was important—practiced hand,
delineating all the things I had done in
that class: puts on galoshes alone, good
at going down the slide, can shovel sand
into a pail—oh, I hope it said these things,
because after that grade everything went
to hell. I valued that card, always, because
it was made with the hand, carefully, and
talked about things I would always care
to remember I had done. And so there were
the events of my baby life, magically recorded
on colored strips of paper carefully pasted
down—my first gift of writing, the beginning
of literature, my first unbound book. It would
be a long time before another writing, or any
work of art, would mean as much.

Irises

My mother's irises
along the southern wall
of our home, planted

before I was born,
lent their fragrance to
my early morning risings,

their yellow and purple faces
opening to the sun.
And throwing open the

window to inhale
the early morning air
I felt their radiance

enter my life.

That Day

What was his name?
Would anyone remember?
He inside the small casket
being carried out by just
two pallbearers.

It must have been a Saturday
or Sunday. We were standing on
the sidewalk, just up from
The Red Cross Drug Store
where I often bought my
comics. Had we attended
the funeral, or were we watching
the procession from the outside,
puzzled, awed, wondering.

He was the first person I had
ever known to die. We were
maybe eight years old, and we
hadn't the feelings to go with
the event. Or the know-how.
We weren't exactly scared, and
we weren't really feeling sad.
Just numb. I don't think we
ever spoke of it again.
It simply passed out of our lives.
As he did. A child's mysterious
death, that, like most everything else,
filled us only with wonder.
And with a sense of loss that
we could not understand.

Island Park

Openly hidden in the middle of our town, where the river stopped, turned around on itself, inhaling once, twice in a loop, before exhaling again in the direction of the factories, tanneries, and bridges of commerce, Island Park was the held breath of grace, the one complete gift of love to the city and its people.

It was there I discovered art and fortunately thought of it neither as discovery or art, but only as wonder—for I saw in man's art his uncontrollable urge to speak intimately with nature, by holding up what he had made to mirror back what he had seen.

For there, at the bottom of Liberty Street, where it entered the park, in the backyard of the house facing the water and bridge, was a rock garden with a bridge that was a replica in miniature of the bridge I had started to cross, and was looking back from now. My first experience of another world, the palpable world of the imagination.

There too, where I first discovered art, I learned about love, and because love came first, everything else followed. It was my earliest memory of life—my father carrying me in his arms along the worn path, with the bushes around and above, stirring under a warm breeze. And another was there, perhaps my uncle, and something moved amongst us, a warm feeling, a feeling of grace, a blessing that I knew to be love.

Under the same bridge, I crabbed for bait for myself, and also to sell to the fishermen on Lake Michigan. The crabbing was best there because of the rocky bottom, where the crabs hid and waited, allowing us to coax them out with pieces of liver tied to butcher string that dangled from a cut branch, all but the latter purchased from the Boranian Grocery Store on State Street. Mr. Boranian would always wrap extra string around the white butcher paper, for he knew where we were headed. We would stand there, silently enraptured by the odors of Armenia that oozed forth from the spices on the shelves, as well as from the opened lentil and bulghour sacks.

The Emperor of Ice Cream

Hear the bell of the ice-cream man jingle
and watch us all run from wherever we are
to wherever he finally stops, letting his foot
fall from the bicycle pedal to the ground
halting his heavy wagon of dry ice
dixie cups popsicles and sammy bars
and watch as he turns his funny hat to
take us on one by one before moving his
magical ice cream show to another block.

No matter what we always had money for ice
cream from the ice-cream man.

Mulberry Trees

When
as a small boy
I saw them ripen against
the early summer sun
I stopped alone for an hour
and ate until my fingers
took an ancient purple stain

until something remembered
a smaller, knotty tree
in a barren, rocky landscape
before an older, quieter sun

and I went home a little
sadder, a little gladdened
and standing on the porch
my mother and father
saw their Armenian son.

Father's Hands

Had your hands been different
when you cooked in the Army,
and later at the Nelson Hotel
in the years before I was born?
Did you yearn to return to that
time, to a profession you never
quite made your own? Or did you
accept your lot as an immigrant
factory worker, who anyhow had
a family, a job, a mortgage, and
a roof over his head. Your factory-
tough hands, with callouses over
callouses. Did you mind? I didn't
know to admire your skills, only
to feel sorry that you were no longer
a practicing chef. I took you at
your word, and of course explaining
and justifying was not your way.
Instead, we fished together on the lake,
whenever I could get you to agree
to rise early on a Saturday, when we'd
walk to the pier, with sandwiches
you made, before preparing the
last minute breakfast I was
almost too excited to eat, in anticipation
of the fishing we would find.
When we fished with crabs you
would stick your hand in the bucket
and bring them out, clinging to your
fingers, banging all but one back into

the pail, while I shuddered in disbelief.
It was strangely heroic, and maybe that's
why it both pleased me and scared me.
Your expression never changed, nor did
you become flustered over my screaming
and hollering and talking, that I mostly did
while also trying to catch the most fish.

The One Day

We want some days to waken again
to that first morning,
when a golden sun shone on the
window's ledge, and with an odor
that was sun and light and morning
and something else—
a something that made you turn to
look and listen as if for the very first time.

Alone and cared for and free and loved,
when your mother was the only girl
you would ever love,
and father would always defend.

Horses

I didn't really want to be
Tom Mix. I wanted to be Tom
Mix's horse. Or did I just
want to see Tom Mix's horse,
with or without Tom Mix riding
on top of him? My father was upset.
He had never taken me to the
movies before. First we saw
the Paramount News, then we waited.
Then we saw the Looney Tunes.
And waited. Finally we saw the
horses come. But they didn't
stay. That's when I screamed.
My father got mad. But we stayed
until the end. I knew he wanted
to take me home.
He didn't care about the horses.
All he cared about was my
screaming. He wanted it to stop.
When we got home he told
mother. Who understood.

I must have forgotten about
horses & cowboys & movies
for awhile,
because the next I remember
I was going to movies by myself,
or with my friends.
Father must have been relieved..

The Fishermen

I do not remember a time when we used the dilapidated garage at the back of our yard. For as long as I can remember, Bill Zaehler, our next door neighbor, rented it from my parents for 50 cents a month. Inside, he kept his minnow and crab tanks, and large fishing nets, that were lined in the back—after being poled out to dry in his long, narrow yard. His backyard was identical in size to ours, but, unlike ours—which was full of trees and vegetables, flowers and a grape arbor—his consisted of struggling patches of grass, flourishing weeds, and a well-worn path between his home and our garage, which faced his yard.

Here, he and his fishing relatives talked, cleaned fish, and dried their nets. The yard belonged, as well, to Bill's dog, Bozo, a mean fox-terrier, who barked at everyone who entered his domain, and never tired of biting my ankles.

He knew of course who belonged to the yard and who did not. But there was another, easier way to get rid of me. "Perch are running, Dave," Bill would say, as I stood, open-mouthed, watching the men pulling perch and trout from their nets.

"They *are*, Uncle Bill," I would answer, incredulous, never suspecting.

"Joe Perch went home an hour ago with a stringer full."

"But he always catches a stringer full, Uncle Bill."

"They're running, Dave! I tell you, they're running. Boys at the weather station say there's a storm blowing in. Winds'll be shifting south any minute. You know what that means."

"Blow the bait into the fish's mouth," I'd answer, and without another word, I'd dash into my back yard and grab my two cane poles, that I kept tied under the rainpipe, where our reclining roof line stopped just above my head.

Did the fish ever once run when Bill said they would? Had he even once been to the pier and watched the fishermen, before coming home and making his pronouncement? And did I ever notice a change in the weather once I got to the pier?

I doubt it, because looking back, I think it was a mutually supportive game. No one could not enjoy teasing a child that was as incredulous as I, and since we both loved fishing, I'm sure he enjoyed seeing me go off—and return—even if I had nothing more to show for my effort than three or four perch.

I can see him now, laughing to himself. His big grin and dancing eyes. He was a good tease—the right kind of tease, because he never laughed at anyone. The joke was life itself, its vagaries and mysteries—and he had let himself in for the ride.

And his grin said: Anyone can be in on it, just join up before life passes by.

My father, too, was a fisherman of sorts.

Perhaps it was he who taught me to fish, but I doubt it.

I was born to fish, and I cannot remember a time when I did not fish. In fact, I date my memory by this fact, because all of my remembrances before I was a fisherman are fuzzy, except for one in particular, which is etched on my soul.

I must have been four years old. We were on our way to the picnic grounds at the end of Lincoln Field. My uncle was driving us in his Model-A Ford, my father beside him, while my mother and I sat quietly in back.

As we entered the park and drove alongside the river, I spotted two fishermen standing in the river, where the water moved back and forth across their knees. They were waving what looked like magic wands, that I knew somehow were magical poles. The river sparkled, reflecting the warm rays of the sun, and rippled as it rushed below the men. It seemed to be blue, white and golden all at once. And I knew in an instant what all of it meant, that there were living beings in the water that these men were trying to catch. But more than the fish, and more than the fishermen, I was spellbound by the water—the ultimate mystery, the life before life, that I was certain now had brought me here.

I was seeing Root River for the very first time.

No substance or meaning would ever enter deeper into the heart of my being. I would follow its course all of my young life, from the State Street bridge, where I next encountered it, to the dam, far outside town—and then, above the dam and beyond, and as I traveled to other rivers and cities, all the rivers became extensions of this river, and all the cities extensions of this city, for the meaning of life had begun for me in the form and ritual of these two fishermen, their lines dripping beads of water, as they whipped their rods up from river's surface and then laid their lines back down.

Saturdays with Father

Do you remember our
walking to the lake together,
those early Saturday summer
mornings, the stillness
at that hour, nothing
but the idle boater
on the river
the occasional car
puttering down the street,
now and then a house light
in somebody's kitchen,
the sun on the invisible
horizon, streaking the sky
in colors of orange and pink

I'd watch my tennies touch
the pavement, the sound of
your work shoes in my ear.
the shuffling crabs,
the cane poles
swinging in my arms,
and in your hands
a cushion & a bucket
that held our lunch
while mine held crabs.

We'd stop at Umbaji Park
and drink at the
bubbling fountain
whose waters tasted

of the brass perforated
ball and the pebbles
it darkened, all of it
bringing to my tongue
the flavor of earth and sky
and breathless air,
until we wandered through
the coal yards and
factories, everything stilled

But for the repeated
blasts of the fog horn
at the end of the pier,
then the smell of the lake,
the dampening air,
my hands twitching
involuntarily
upon the poles

I'd kick a pebble
and hoot,
and you'd tell me what
I already knew
that soon we would
be there
would be there

Windows

The best part of school
was the window I looked
out of—over the seen
and imagined spaces
there and beyond

The school bell never sounded
or announced its arrival
inside my head

I heard only the trees
and birds singing
and what the wind said

Across the schoolyard
tenement noises
with cars passing
and talking trucks
everywhere

The rag and tin man
on his horse-driven cart
and the excited fireman's
clang   clang   clang

Outdoors

Outdoors. That's where my childhood was lived. Looking out of windows caused me to remain in school two years longer than I should have. I even flunked the fifth grade twice—the second time in summer school: a torture for which my budding spirit was unprepared. I balanced the fault, if not the outrage, by quitting two years before I would have graduated from high school.

Everything took my eye to the window, and then, when spring arrived, nothing could take my eye away. The dull classroom, the dull teacher, and my fellow inmates—I was never able to understand how we had fallen into such a condition.

I had one of two major choices once I left the indoors: Root River or Lake Michigan. When not walking to the lake, usually alone, I would ride to Root River on my bike with two cane poles and a bucket containing a stringer and a small can of worms.

If I rode up State Street, as I often did, I would pass Dedeh sitting in front of our church, and this would fill me with shame, not only for myself, but also for him, because he, too, seemed shabby and without dignity, as he sat alone all day, involved in something as incomprehensible to me as I was sure my fishing was to everyone else.

But the drive to go fishing was strong. I wonder now if it wasn't melancholy, and that the sadness I carried within was lodged so deep in my spirit, that I was unaware of this at the time, and that I inexplicably experienced only as shame.

Our Sparrows

The tall, very tall yellow brick chimney
aged into darkness by soot and time
that stood down below the end
of our dead-end street
beside the woodwork factory it served—
held, in its four tiny squared apertures
near the top (made by the removal or
absence of one or at most two of the bricks),
the homes of many sparrows;
and always, coming home, or just standing
on the porch, I would look up
and see them flying in and out,
or just perched there, waiting and watching
before leaping into flight.

We are known by what we remember,
what we noticed.
Each poet must find his own objects
in the sun.
And so I remember this
as something of significant beauty
that is gratefully beyond the need
of any words
although words must sometimes be used
to indicate the real.

The chimney, the little window openings,
and the sparrows that made of it their home,
were simply there, mingling
their time with ours,

and this is what time meant:
the keeping of the rituals of the eyes
and heart.

Sparrows would always be my only nightingales.

Pantries

Years later I heard from my mother
of the pantry in the old country
where all the foodstuffs of the
several families were kept—damp
and cold with the mingled odors of
shelves and hanging foods, and it
must have been to there that I
traveled in your walk-in pantry,
Zary, in your La Salle Street home,
smaller than my grandmother's pantry
but larger than any other in these
new Armenian homes, and now I am
remembering the hours I stood in
there looking at shelves of food
turning, wondering and remembering—
I knew not what.

Home

The door leading to the cellar
was off the kitchen. One door
opened, my father entered,
then the other door opened
to accept his heavy gray coat
before he descended the stairs
to the makeshift shower below
to wash the factory dirt
from his pores, before rising
clean to the kitchen
where we stood or sat
a small family gathered
against the shifting weight
of the world and its fortunes
that did not include us in its design.

Remember
for Mikey Kaiserlian

Remember the living stream
Island Park where we went
with our bicycles for walks
or games under the ballpark light
the bubbling fountains the rock
garden bridge by the bridge
where we entered the park
the pavilion so mighty brown
and proud with long veranda
to hold the dancing throng
and the bridge that led out
from there to everywhere
our city at night under the moon
and the rows of park lights near
where the fireflies made their
own light while we moved
among bushes and lanes at one
with everything that lived
children in search of life

The Coffee House
for Naz Gengozian

It seemed fitting that it
was unpainted, unwashed,
uncared for and neglected
and therefore a perfect haunt
for the Armenians from
the other side

A coffee house, or *sourjarran*,
in the old country language
from where they had
lately come

Inside that singular space
beyond what the name foretold
was something more than
backgammon board & dice

There, outside the fenced-in
enclosure of Garfield School,
with us too frightened
to ever enter inside

Our curiosity sated by
the stolen glance, the
furtive look into that large
smoke-filled room
The inhabitants dressed
in grays and browns,

somber, silent, belonging
to a world outside of ours

That was somehow also ours
for these were our fathers,
the other half
of the split-off world

We knew only as Armenia,
a name and a tragedy
they could revisit, but that we
dared not enter with our lives

The Birthday

Everybody brought $1.00 to give
Dom Galati for his birthday,
if they didn't bring him a present
instead. Not me. I brought 50 cents.
That was what my mother gave me
to bring. We argued. She won.
I knew $1.00 was the right amount.
From such decisions as hers
lifelong embarrassments were born.

The Accident

It was the apples that made
me appreciate that experience,
looking back on that day
when the man with a bag full
started down our dead end
street steps and before we
knew what had happened,
ended up at the bottom,
with a hole in his head.

That's how we spoke of it later
when we remembered the man
with the hole-in-his-head,
but what it actually looked
like I can no longer say.
We all gathered at the foot
of the stairs and watched
the ambulance carry him away,
alive, but frightened as I
had never seen anyone
frightened before.

And then Father gathered
up the apples and we all
went home.

Dedeh

Dedeh, I was to find out much later, meant Grandfather in Turkish. It could also mean Father of the race, in which case the name could be taken as a title, or as an earned honor—an acquired name that effaced the given name of the man.

I was not aware of it at the time, but Dedeh, I am sure, had been named in this way.

He was in no way noble or outstanding. Nor was he distinguished, or in any way special. And yet, as the accumulation of lived moments, coalesce and pass gradually into memory, what emerges from my own remembrance, is a man who possessed all of these qualities, along with the still greater quality of humility.

He was, I believe now, all of these things because he was none of them. He was none of them because he thought of himself as nothing. I don't think he even thought of himself as simple or unimportant. Perhaps he thought of himself as insignificant.

It was because of this right attitude—that is possessed by so few, and understood and valued by even fewer—that he was able to find his function, which he had assumed, I am sure, without appointment, and had fulfilled without any special thanks.

I don't remember if I ever spoke to him, but whenever I rode my bike up State Street, he would be there, sitting on his metal folding chair, mornings and afternoons, in front of the doors off St. Mesrob Armenian Church.

Traveling west from home, I would pass first the fire station and wave to the blue uniformed firemen, sitting in threes and fours on their sturdy wooden chairs. They would wave back and call out, and I would be proud to be recognized by men whose badges flashed so brilliantly in the sun.

And then, just next door, I would see Dedeh again, in his old clothes, seated, serene and silent, and I would look away and bicycle on.

Sundays he would stand in front of the church and enter with the last of the parishioners. But all week he kept his vigil alone, nodding to his countrymen as they passed, as he did to those who occasionally entered the doors he sat beside.

The meek shall inherit the earth, the Bible says. Dedeh had inherited his portion of it while he lived.

He grows more understandable and cherishable with each passing year.

To My Father

When I think of the Tseffos bakery
I always think of you. Perhaps it has
to do with bread, the staff of life,
the one simple staple without which
it seems there could be no meaningful life.

The one thing the Armenians didn't sell
or make themselves, was their own
peda bread, since it was already being
made by the Greek family that lived
above their bakery on Douglas Avenue

where we went every Sunday morning
to bring their freshly baked peda
to our homes. It was the tradition,
the worn, familiar, weekly ritual
without which our simple lives would

not have been complete. We'd slice it
for sandwiches, or to eat with our soup,
or to dip into the yogurt dish with, or,
best of all, to stuff with our kebabs,
especially at picnics, along with the

barbecued pepper, tomatoes, and the
marinated onions that gave it its special
flavor and life. The peda was us,
it was our family, and it was me and you,
together or alone, walking the four or
five blocks to bring it home once again,

because a Sunday without it—and for
as long as it stretched into the week—
would have made the transition from
old country to new too unbearable for you

and much too confusing for me,
because I needed what was old as much
as what was new, even if I didn't
fully understand this at the time.

The Nights

It was the glistening light
of night that we walked in,
slightly atremble, our shoe
shine boxes in hand, cruising
Douglas Avenue in pairs, some-
times shouting our holdings
and findings and plans to
the other roving pairs—
but never our fears, unaware
of our bravery, entering taverns
sometimes alone, making no
more than a dollar or two
for the night, but we were
learning—what exactly we did
not know, except that the
money earned was ours to do
with as we wished, allowing
us to make plans, to prepare
for future wants and needs,
knowing we could do something
for ourselves, however small,
and all of this gave us a
certain pride which balanced
out the inferior feelings that
the work instilled—for work
it was, and it was manhood we
were slowly entering, inching
along that avenue, lost and alone
in the all-American midwestern night.

The Pond

We sat all day on that pond
in our borrowed row boat,
the first time that way
my father and I, silently
fishing as if on holiday—

We must have been visiting
mother's friends, who could
have lived nearby, lending
us their boat for the afternoon,
if that's when it was—

And then when it was over,
when we pulled up our poles,
we were surprised to find
a golden-bellied sunfish
on father's line.

We stayed a little longer
because of that, but that
was all we saw or caught
and all that stands out for the
telling, but for the memory

I keep of the two of us there
on that pond, the first time
fishing that way, a father and a son
being father and son, as if words
could convey what that meant to my heart.

Harry Gaykian

We were playing in your back
yard when it happened.
It came over the radio,
but I can't remember,
did we hear the radio
from the back yard,
or did your mother or sister Sue
come out and make the announcement:
President Roosevelt is dead!

We were stunned. No one we knew
had ever died before.
Could this happen to our President?
We stared at each other,
unable to speak or move.
But we believed it,
we knew it was true,
and yet its meaning
was beyond us, completely
beyond our childhood reach.

He was the father of our country,
and now he was gone.
I had to go home.
There was nothing else to do.
Our play had forever ended,
because soon after that you moved
with your family to California.
It was the first time
I had lost a friend in that way,

and forever after that loss
was connected in my mind
with the loss of our leader,
and also with that radio,
that radio
that once took our President away.

Parks and the River

The parks gave us what nothing
else could provide:
the anticipation of fireworks
at Washington Park
there upon the golf course lawn,
the streets winding around
the river park, dissecting the bordering bridges
before that river curled back on itself
then flowed onward to that
other park called Lincoln
that I can look back on now
from above, as if the city
had been made from there

While I enter solemnly the kingdom
of lawns and trees & moving water
beside leaves of grass,
and those brick-lined passageways
over which my feet first roamed—
that shielded arbor between sloping hill
and river, dipping down and up
with our bikes following the same paths
we first walked with cane poles in hand,
and again the same weaving bodies
of T-shirted boys, with trunks
under their pants, or yet bare-
bottomed, diving off the trees
that swooned over those mud-
brown banks

Above Island Park

The song I learned & hummed
    & taught Howie
lasted all afternoon
    by the river
until the sun began to set
    & we wandered home
along the bank
    over the bridge
along the streets
    to our summer-quiet homes;
my father on the porch
    waiting,
my mother quietly turning
    in the kitchen
reheating
    the cold food.

Baseball & Father

I saw him coming up the block
and hesitated at the plate,
while he drew nearer & nearer,
that funny pleased-with-himself
smile on his face, wanting to tease
because that was how he loved,
then motioning to the pitcher for the ball,
who lobbed it self-consciously over to him—

But he missed the easy catch, and then
threw the ball awkwardly upward
in the direction of the sky—missing
everyone—but pleased, as if he had
just committed an object of wonder
to the truth of the air

Teaching me—and I alone
understood—that he had joined
our game and had approved;
and then he continued on his way,
his old country walk moving
him through pastures of wonder
and strife, unseen by me
and as yet outside my caring.

Uncle Jack

The stigma of tuberculosis—which was considered at the time to be a fatal disease—was so great that I had always believed Uncle Jack had been gassed in the war, and was therefore unable to work and had to live on his Army pension.

This was the family version of his illness.

We lived the length of our block apart. Ours was the second to last house on the north side of Superior Street, and Uncle Jack's the first house (behind the church, that belonged to State Street) on the south side of the street.

Uncle Jack was a bachelor. I believed he could not marry because of his illness. He stayed at home most of the day, and from the very beginning of my life he was as much a father to me as he was an uncle. Unlike my father, he was calm and patient, and I never once heard him holler or lose his temper.

Also, he didn't take me for granted.

My visits to his home meant as much to him as they did to me.

If I cut my finger open (as I did once, throwing bottles against a brick building on La Salle Street with Mikey Kaiserlian), I went straight to his home, to be bandaged and fed—usually a peanut butter and jelly sandwich. Or if I stepped on a nail (as I did once), I would be carried to his home by Mikey's big brother, Hart. Again, food and sympathy.

In fact, I didn't have to hurt myself to receive his undivided attention.

To know that I had someone to turn to when I was hurt and in danger, was a great comfort and solace to me. It was much better than going home, where I would get loved, scolded and fed— because Uncle Jack left out the scolding part. And his love was always as free as his sandwiches.

"Ha, Tavit, it's you," he would say, opening wide his door.

"Again you have hurt yourself, vy, vy, vy. Come in, come in."

Or we would sit on his back porch steps, overlooking his garden of cherry trees and growing vegetables. For as long as I could remember he lived on the second floor and rented the floor below.

The birds were always eating his cherries.

They must have been more than a common nuisance, because one day he went out and bought a bee-bee gun and began shooting at them. I should emphasize *at them*, because although he taught me how to shoot, as well, and gave me a turn at shooting *at* them, we never loosened a feather on a single bird that I can remember.

I think it was because he refused to leave his perch on the back porch, which was a good twenty yards away from the nearest tree.

"Son a ba gun, birds," he would say. "Vhy dey don't go boder Veber, his trees, ha?" Weber was his sour-faced next door neighbor." Vhat so sweet about Uncle Jack's cherries, can you answer me that?"

I think he was proud that his trees attracted so many birds. I think he liked having his garden sung in all day long by creatures that could fly. It gave him something to complain about.

He didn't like taking things sitting down.

Like all of the other Armenians I knew, he felt cheated by fate, and believed he needed to do something about it.

In the old country, from the age of five, they began putting him on a mule to take food to the workers in the field.

One day, a branch of his family—the Kherdians of Kharpet— were passing along the road on which Uncle Jack was traveling with his mule. They were the first members of the family to take the Turkish threats seriously, and were fleeing for their lives. When they saw their young relative, they invited him along (by now he was ten years old) and without giving it very much thought, he joined them.

He never saw Kharpet again. All of the members of his family, with the exception of his cousin, Yeghnar, were wiped out by the Turks.

50

He only told one story from that time: the story of how he took food to the workers in the field on his donkey. And then, having said that much, he would break down and cry like a baby.

I don't think he understood his regret. I don't think he understood his life. What man does.

In Father's Garden

I never understood that you
wanted me to spade the garden
with you so we could share
that garden's work: the pleasure,
the joy, of growing food all
by ourselves, the two of us
together in our own backyard,
Mother in the grape arbor
with work of her own.

No, I thought you wanted my help.
And this I was reluctant to give
because none of it interested me
at the time.

This chance for us to meet in this way
was missed. Because it didn't work
out like that, it works out now
like this; conjuring you in a poem
while entering that garden again,
willingly turning the earth by your
side, watching as you stop to wipe
your brow, staring into space, sighing,
remembering the past,
your homeland, your
fatherland,
what you missed
that I long for now in you.

United States Tony

United States Tony
was such a man
that amused factory workers
on the home-going bus
by dancing in the aisle
while another man sang;
Never able
to let life lie
one day he invited
his Armenian friend
to a theft of pears
from a farmer's orchard
on the way to the Cudahy Fair;

Promptly caught and challenged
he laughingly replied
(circling the tree
and clapping his hands)
No! No! You can't arrest
me, I'm United States Tony;
No! No! You can't arrest me,
I'm United States Tony.

That aura he carried
circled and danced
and went with him
all the places he went;

And true to the prediction
he had made in the past

he died before drawing
his first pension check

And died with his name
and his life intact.

Herbert Von Haden

Our grab bag lives were cluttered by great mixtures of types and ethnic groups, with their varying predispositions; but the common, undeniable ingredient was poverty—poverty of means, but not of spirit.

But the spirit cannot soar if it is bound by serious physical or material limitations. Instead of soaring, the spirit remains cramped and coarse. We, the Armenians, suffered the further limitation of being the offspring of peasant immigrants, whereas the "Americans" were simple and undeniably coarse, for reasons I was unprepared to understand at the time.

Under these confused and conflicting circumstances, the teachers took to hating, despising, or, at best, condescending to the Armenian children. We didn't speak English the way the other children did—it being, after all, our second language, for Armenian was the only language spoken in most of our homes. And we had strange, unpronounceable names, that we were all too eager to forfeit, if it would do any good—all the while hating our parents for having made such a blunder in the first place. Because my name was David, I received the obverse of this prejudice—the other Armenian children began calling me by the Armenian version of my name— Tavit—and this name was soon taken up by the others, so that I too was made to suffer from a similar embarrassment.

The fact that we were proud and arrogant made it even worse. Who did we think we were to be disdainful of those who con- descended to correct us, and who were working as mercifully as possible to deliver us into the gracious world of Anglo-Saxon America. Into this strange malaise and mixture strode our new principal, Herbert Von Haden, all six feet, six inches of him, in his dark, pinstriped suits, bow ties, and black, pointed shoes.

Not once, not ever, did he look down on us because we were a little backward in our manners, smelled of garlic, wore hand-me-down clothes, were shy and fearful (of authority, in particular), spoke English with a strange idiomatic twist, and often got to the top by pushing a little harder than everyone else.

I think he liked us because we *were* achievers, because we *had* in abundance what he too had in abundance—vitality and an uncontrollable emotional center.

In his own way he exploded as often as we did, and although our respect for him bordered on awe (because he respected us in return), it wasn't this that made us accept his outbursts without question, but rather that his outbursts were no different than our own, except that he had the authority and ability to push what he believed and desired into completion.

Once, for example, he literally kicked Lotch Oglanian off the bench and into our basketball game at Douglas Park, because we were behind in a game we could not afford to lose. That kick alone may have been the reason we won that game. He was more frightening than the opposition, but since we had nothing really to fear in him we had nothing to fear in either the opposition or ourselves.

He made us believe we were okay. And all at once he neutralized the warring forces that were, of course, nothing more than the anxieties everyone felt—from teachers to pupils to parents to leaders, or semi-leaders—because none of us were quite at home where we were, and it was natural to feel that something or someone was at fault. But the force of his presence had made a kind of grace, and brought an understanding that he alone was responsible for.

And then, just as suddenly as he had arrived, he was gone.

A benevolent tornado had come and gone, leaving in its wake a great hole that we would have to fill by ourselves. But he had left us with the means and the confidence that we could.

II

Vision

The seagulls traveling over my head
leaving the home they belonged to—
that lake in the distance, far beyond

The river bridge I stood upon,
peering down the muddy, turgid waters
that emptied into that blue horizon . . .

Where was home, down river with the
wheeling gulls, or toward that open
water that led away under a gallant sun.

Couldn't I slip as easily, tunneling down
that surreptitious weed-choked, stump-
rooted river whose crevices held mysteries

A lifetime of acquainting.

The Song

The rag man calling from
his horse-drawn wagon

the tingling bell
of the ice-cream man

the sharp pincers on ice
heaved over burlapped shoulders

of the grunting ice-men
coming up stairs

the bicycle-propelled
scissor and knife-sharpening man

there on the sidewalk of
our summery home

the blacksmith on the
block below hammering

his black apron
deflecting orange sparks

the reverberating sounds
in the city that once embodied me

the people whose poems
became my life

Root River

where we camped
above where the
river turned
the huge oak
spread its roots
deep in the still water
where the black bass
hid
and where we
fished for them
in the morning

peering straight
down
from the tree's trunk
to where they hid
in the shadows
and considered
our bait

Calling My Name

Remember when
Superior Street
held the world
swaying in its arms
wafting innocence
for miles
down that block
elm trees and fences
to carve & kiss behind

brother of many names
sisters in the night
come now and add your
incense to the hour
while I sing of a lost
child's fireflies.

For Nazeli

The little girl stood on
the tiny cement stoop
on the corner of La Salle
and Jackson Streets,
from where she could
see the approaching boys—

Nobody knew why she would
want to see the boys from
an extra distance, grow
frightened and run for home—

And nobody knew why this
tiny block of cement was
placed just there, having a
function only children
could invent—

Nobody knew, nobody knew—
and the little girl is
still perched there, and
boys are approaching from
everywhere.

Joe Perch

Our Joe Perch was every fisherman's hero on the pier at North Beach.

He had his method and his system, but I didn't have either of those things, nor was I looking to find them. What I wanted was a secret, because if I could find the secret then it would be mine alone, and a secret was a lot easier to guard than a method or a system. Also, it was more mysterious than art, and much more certain than science. That was how I saw it, anyhow.

If I had had brothers and sisters, like all of my other friends, I might not have been in my imagination as much. Not that I thought that made me peculiar. If anything made me peculiar it was that when I got interested in something I went all out for whatever it was and dropped everything else. This, and not having brothers and sisters, was what made me a loner. I always wanted to get to the bottom of things. But only if I was interested. Because it was only when you got to the bottom of something that you found the secret, and then you weren't just *in* something, that thing was also in *you*. And when that happened you weren't lonely or apart any more.

That's probably not the way it was with Joe Perch. He was cool and detached.

And perfect!

I wanted to be like that on the outside, even though I knew I could never be like that on the inside. But then again maybe I *could* be both. Also, I knew that whether Joe Perch was really a scientist or an artist, one thing was certain, he had the secret. Even if he didn't know he had it, he still had it. What would it take for me to acquire a secret that would be mine alone?

I had already tried imitating Joe—but that didn't work. The fact that I didn't like fishing the way Joe did didn't really matter, because if I had caught fish his way it wouldn't have taken any time for me to change my mind. I liked to fish far out on the pier, to be near the fog horn, from where I could look far out on the lake and dream about things I had never seen, and places where I had never been. And I liked being where the water was deep, where I could imagine the big fish lurked, even though it was extremely rare to catch a jumbo perch anywhere on the pier—that is, one weighing a half pound or more. A jumbo perch was a prize that was at least equal in my mind to a whole stringer of fish. I could imagine my pole bending in half, wondering if it would hold, and how old my fish was and how many lines he had broken, and all the time I was hauling him in, thinking maybe he was record size, and even before he broke water, thinking of all the people I would show my jumbo to, and that maybe I'd even get my picture in the paper.

This was still a dream because I hadn't caught my first jumbo.

Meanwhile, I kept remembering the one that got away. He didn't break my line or pole, he just got off the hook. But I knew he was a monster because he was so heavy, and it took all I had just to get him up a few feet, which was only a few seconds after I actually had him on.

The other thing about fishing far out on the pier was that you could jig your line up and down to entice the fish, which I needed to do because I was too impatient to just sit and wait for them to come to me on their own. They said you could catch herring that way, but I didn't know if they were right about that. I had only caught two herring in my whole life, once by jigging and once not. Herring, because of their elongated shape were bigger looking than most jumbo perch, but they weren't prized. The reason was they had worms in their gills, and probably in their stomachs, as well, and since everyone counted on eating their fish, because we were all kind of poor, herring just weren't as sought after as perch. Also, they were harder to catch, and that was probably the real reason. Whether they went for jigged bait or not I didn't know, but I did know that they often came to the surface, and not only for dead minnows, but also for match sticks, that they took for minnows. Whenever that happened I would pull my minnow up to the surface to entice them, but of course it always sank, and so that never worked. If there was a secret to catching herring I didn't know what it was. Nobody did.

Another reason I liked fishing far out on the pier was that you could drop your bucket down into the water whenever you were thirsty and have a free drink, because the water of Lake Michigan was so deep and clear and cold. After awhile, some of the kids would come around that worked for old man Cook, who had a shanty at the end of the pier, where he sold soft drinks, and stuff, as well as minnows, and sometimes crabs. He also rented poles. If I ever had any money I could buy a soda pop or a candy bar. But just as important, I could get news about how everyone was doing, and if they were biting better in one place than another, and whether on the harbor side or not. Of course Joe Perch was always filling up his stringer, and no one ever gave you any news without first giving you the news about Joe Perch, who was everyone's hero on the pier.

Unlike most of the rest of us, Joe Perch fished close in, where the water was no more than five or six feet deep, and where you could practically see to the bottom, except that there were jagged rocks everywhere that had been put there to shore up the pier. Joe Perch was the only fisherman who didn't put sinkers on his line. He was also the only one to use bobbers, and his bobbers were unique, being made from wine bottle corks, and secured to the line with match sticks. I had this theory that the reason he used match sticks—which protruded above the corks—was because the change in the angle of the match stick when the perch struck had everything to do with where the perch was in relation to the hook: just nibbling on the minnow, running with it, chewing it slowly, or swallowing it. He probably had that part of it down to a science. The art of it was that he could have thought of such a thing in the first place.

All the rest of us hooked our minnows behind the neck and up through the gills. But not Joe. He hooked his minnows through the back and under the spine, so they would stay alive and even struggle to swim once he lowered them into the water. This is probably what drove the fish crazy. Because he didn't have any sinkers on his lines, and because the rocks made the water choppy, his minnows would sometimes come floating up near the surface. Whenever that happened a fish came up and took the bait. It drove me wild. I wanted more than anything to see my bait and watch the fish come after it, and also to know where they hid, how they behaved, and all the rest of it. But I just couldn't duplicate what Joe did. Nobody could. We had all sat near him at one time or another and tried to copy his methods, but it never worked. In fact, there were always some new imitators on each side of Joe Perch whenever you walked by him, but they never lasted long. The way I looked at it Joe's method was something you couldn't imitate. It was something you had to admire, and just leave it at that.

I finally came to the conclusion that the way Joe Perch fished was all wrong for me. I was too rambunctious and impatient. Joe Perch would wait all day if he had to, because he knew what he was waiting for. But I was still trying to find out—about everything. What I didn't realize right away was that finding out about things was half the fun, and maybe *all* of the fun. I needed to learn things, and the only way to learn was by trial and error. For one thing, Joe Perch always fished with minnows, but probably half the guys on the pier used crabs. Since I could never afford to buy minnows, I had to go out and catch my own crabs on Root River. The river was too muddy to catch the crabs by hand, so I used liver that I bought for a nickel at Boranian's Grocery Store on State Street. I would use the string that old man Boranian used to tie up the package with, and when I got to the river I'd break a stick from a bush, and I'd be in business.

Sometimes I would trade some of my crabs for minnows when I got to the pier, or even sell a dozen of them and turn around and buy minnows. I also learned how to cut fish bait. And because I also fished on the river I had learned how to catch night crawlers with a flashlight at night. So I was learning a lot of things, and each of these things was exciting in itself.

But this didn't mean that Joe Perch didn't go on being my idol. It's just that I was beginning to realize that it was just as valuable to be myself as it was to find someone to admire and learn from and look up to. And it didn't really matter that I didn't understand everything there was to know about Joe Perch. What mattered was that, where fishing was concerned, there was someone out there who had mastered it, and went about his work without wasted motion, in complete control of his thoughts and feelings. It felt good to know he was there, even if he never spoke, even if he didn't know I existed.

The months came and went, and then one day, when the fishing was slow, as usual, and I was wondering if the six perch I had caught would make a meal for our family, I suddenly felt the familiar bam-bam of a perch strike, but this time when I set the hook it felt like I had snagged a rock. And then the pole began to pull away from me—as if I had a torpedo on the other end. That was when I knew I had a jumbo. Instead of pulling with all my might, as I always imagined I would do if I had a jumbo on the line, I eased the fish as best I could, and then let him run, and then eased him up again, and then let him run again, and back and forth like that—easy, easy, easy, and all along I knew exactly what to do, until inch by inch I brought him up, and watched him break the surface and come gliding toward me under my control.

The next thing I knew a shout began to chorus from one end of the pier to the other: "Jumbo . . . Jumbo . . . Jumbo!" But this time—for the first time—I wasn't part of the chorus, because it was me and my fish that were being cheered.

I just couldn't fish after that. It was the happiest moment of my life as a fisherman. And it meant that I *was* a fisherman. Not a master, not an artist or scientist, and not even a champion. But a fisherman, real and true.

When I passed Joe Perch on my way down the pier, I wanted

more than anything to flash my jumbo in front of his eyes, but I had too much pride for that. Instead, I looked down at his stringer of perch floating out from the pier and congratulated him, as I always did, hoping to get a word or two out of him, which of course had never happened. But this time he turned and looked at me, and then down at my jumbo that was on the stringer I was holding in front of me. "That's a real jumbo you got there, son," he said.

"I was out at the end of the pier jigging a minnow," I said, as casually as I possibly could. "Uhm," he said, but he didn't look out to the end of the pier where I had caught my fish, nor did he look out over the water to give the vast lake or the setting sun some thought, either. Instead, he turned back to his bobbing corks, waiting for the match sticks to twitch, or the corks to disappear under water.

He had given me all the time he could afford. Joe Perch was all business. And his business was catching fish. I wondered what my business would be, and if I would ever find it, and most important of all, if I would be as good at what I did as Joe Perch was at what he did, which was catching more fish than anyone else, and without any seeming effort.

He was an artist all right, and some day, I figured, I would be some kind of artist myself.

Foundry

In the distance the drop
forge hammer resounds, and
then an orange glow, strangely
luminescent, blossoms
before us as we walk along,
skirting the coal yards
and the foundries,
traveling the wobbly factory bridge
toward the bright lights
of the city beyond.

Father

When you put on your black
shoulder-strapped bathing suit
you became somehow
even more Armenian than
you were before.
I watched you enter
the water, swim
by yourself,
and then slowly return,
somehow separated
from the general surround.

I stood on the beach with
mother—or alone—
and watched you, strangely suited,
making even the water you stood in
seem foreign, forlorn.

The Bins

Playing by night was not the same as playing by day. The games were different, and different still the moods of the night and the sounds.

My solitary flight had ended—for all day I would be alone on Root River, or, occasionally, Lake Michigan. After supper, and after dark had set in, I would leave the house to play with the gang, who converged from the neighboring streets, as well as from our own: La Salle, Jackson, Prospect, and Superior—always a good block to play on because of the abandoned factory across the street from my house, where hardly a window remained to be broken, and the woodwork factory it joined, with its flat, easy-to-climb roof; but with low hanging wires that left both Jerry Hansen and me with permanent scars on our foreheads; and its bins, where the remains of paint and lacquer cans and chemicals were dumped or discarded.

The three bins, which bordered the factory, were cement-walled and partitioned, and ran perhaps halfway down the length of Superior Street at its dead end.

These bins, perhaps as self-protection, were sealed off by an easy-to-climb red wooden fence. And it was here, gagging on the mixed metallic and acidic stink of the refuse in the bins, that I inhaled my first cigarette. I took a sudden jolt. It felt like the kick of a mule, but with this difference: the mule was inside of me and trying to get out. It was a strange experience, unprepared for, unexpected; a ritual practiced by all the youth of my generation, but not commonplace on that account or for that reason.

Later, we smoked in the back seat of the Model A parked in Zaehler's back yard. It must have been a junker. It was parked not fifty yards from the back of my house. I had this certain sense that my mother knew (but chose not to reveal that she knew) that I was out there with one of my buddies, secretly smoking up a storm.

The Crab & Minnow Bait Garages
for Bill Zaehler, Jr.

This was my idea of what a business
should be and could be if it was run
by someone who was in possession

of his life. For once, such a garage had
been ours, but it was so worn, lopsided
and dilapidated that it wasn't good

for anything, but maybe Father's
gardening tools, and so Mother rented
it to our neighbor, Bill Zaehler, for fifty

cents a month. He put in minnow
tanks and large buckets for crabs and
night crawlers, with a contraption

that kept the water moving, creating
oxygen for the living minnows
he sold for a quarter a dozen, though
I don't recall ever seeing a customer
cough up any such coin, or even make
an entrance into that holy shrine

where I hung out whenever I could
along with Bill's nephews, who were
my buddies and his helpmates, and so

all in all it looked to me like the greatest
American enterprise imaginable, with
a future as bright and as certain as was

the sorrow that brooded on our side
of the fence, where we were housing the
past, while inching towards our own

New America, over which my imagination
wandered, my eyes on the nets poled out
for drying in their yard, their dog Bozo

keeping me at bay, sensing my foreignness
and my fear, my inability to insinuate myself
into the easy ways of his master and his

cohorts—those casual designers of milieus
and dramas American; vast unending
panoramas of casual sense

Hovhannes Pahltahlian

I am sure there was a lore that went with every one of the tiny parks that dotted our city, but the park and its lore that was also somehow a part of my own lore was Umbaji Park.

Umbaji, whose name meant foreman in Turkish, was an Armenian.

Colbert was the official name of the park, but it had never been called that as far as I know, although I can remember a time when it was called Bum's Park. That must have been before Umbaji took up full-time residence.

It was located at the end of Prospect Street, which was the street at the bottom of our dead end block. From the bottom of Superior Street—below where it dead ended—Prospect Street ran for another half block to Douglas Avenue, and then another short block—with the entire north side of the street being occupied by St. Patrick's Church—where it ended at Umbaji Park.

Sitting on a knoll, in the shadow of St. Patrick's Church, Umbaji Park overlooked the State Street and Main Street bridges, and—in the distance—Lake Michigan. It was a tiny park that sloped at a 45 degree angle, and it was shaped in a triangle. The one bench—that Umbaji freely moved about—was often at the top of the park, from where it commanded a full view of all that I have described.

At the bottom of the hill there was a drinking fountain bordering the sidewalk, and a low tubular fence and shrub bushes, as protection, because the park at this point was built above the street, there being no sidewalk at the base of the "triangle."

Because of the way it was situated, it provided a commanding view of the city, the river, and of the populace—as it passed by foot and car and boat.

But I don't think Umbaji chose his park for any of these reasons.

He had come to Racine in 1910 to make money to return to the homeland with, as so many Armenians before him had done. He was unable to return because of the war, and when his wife was killed in the Armenian Massacres, he was too old to start another life in America. With no home or promise or future, he came in time to make this tiny, insignificant park his final resting place.

His name, I found out much later, was Hovhannes Pahltahlian, and, like my father, he was from Adana, although his ancestors had come from Tomarza, as my father's had come from Kharpet.

Although I saw him several times a week during the summer months, I don't believe I ever heard him speak.

It was said he washed his clothes in the fountain, slept on the bench, and relieved himself in the bushes. This was the lore of the park—a legend created by children and later perpetuated by adults.

But I had been there as a witness to the man, not the legend.

Walking to Lake Michigan in the early morning, cane poles in one hand, a bucket of crabs in the other, I always stopped for a drink at the fountain, the water fresh, clean and cold, as it bubbled ceaselessly over the perforated brass ball, and tumbled over tiny pebbles of white and brown. While I drank I stared at the pebbles and inhaled the aroma of the fountain, its damp, cool smell seeming to be the earthy soul of the fountain itself.

Umbaji was always in sight, sitting or lying on his bench, mute, listless, and gray. I knew he was Armenian, I knew he had no work, and I knew very little else.

I would straighten from the fountain, bang my poles on the sidewalk to align their bottoms, turn and go on my way.

Chuck Pehlivanian

We had certain lunacies in common,
but the one I remember best was the
idea of digging our own fish pond
in your family's backyard. We went
so far as to consult Old Man Cook,
who ran the bait shack by the pier.

He wasn't the first one to laugh at us,
but he was the only one who took the
trouble to explain why it wouldn't work:
no running water meant no oxygen, and
even if the fish survived they'd soon
be swimming in their own shit.

Never mind. We decided to build a boat
instead. At this point our mothers
brought our fathers into the act.
Your dad had a car—very unusual—
and together they took us fishing.
We supplied the gear and enthusiasm,
they got to provide everything else.

None of us knew where to go or what
to do once we got there. I think they
figured we couldn't all fish out of
one boat without at least three of us
drowning. And so, not finding a place
to fish at Brown's Lake, we worked our
way back towards town, finally settling
for a tiny pond at Johnson's Park.

There was this big concern over the minnows
that kept splashing on the floor in back.
First one of our dads, and then the other
would turn around and say, "Watch it out
the minnets," or, "Be careful, don't spill
it, the winnets."Neither one of them
could speak English worth a damn.

They dropped us off and went searching
for grape leaves, figuring we'd only
get wet, and maybe decide to quit.
The pond wasn't deep enough to drown
a good sized fish. We made a game of
throwing first the winnets and then the
minnets into the pond, imitating their
accents, and then cracking up and falling
to the ground.

We didn't catch a single fish, and they
didn't do much better with grape leaves.
We were wet and miserable driving home,
and they were sad and disgusted—but also
relieved to have it done. We drove back
in silence, staring out our private windows,
filling the landscape with our different
dreams and losses.

Your father broke the silence with a sigh,
saying, simply, "Where we are. Where we are,"
meaning, not this ordinary day with its
ordinary losses, but the time of his life,

that had taken him all the way here,
America, from all the way there, Armenia,
the bewildering and inexplicable passage
of our mysterious life on earth.

Yo-Yos

The grocery store lady across from
Washington Junior High, I am sure,
hired the Filipinos who came in
the spring, just before school closing
to show us the tricks they knew to do
with their Yo-Yos, making them walk,
twirling and sending them in porch swing
loops, and then making them stop in midair.
And back up. And stuff like that. They
never spoke. They didn't have to.
They just showed their tricks.
And then the old lady came out and
sold us Yo-Yos just like theirs.

Dominic Galati

You were my only connection with Italian town,
but our friendship was such that it wasn't long
before your neighborhood was nearly as familiar
to me as my own.

We played basketball together, using the hoop
over your garage, and sometimes watched Mike
Bencriscutto, the golf pro, chipping with his
wedge in the front yard across from your house.

I liked the different smells of the grocery store
on your block, and I began to see that your people
and my people had come from a common lot:
the immigrants who labored, and because they did,
helped to make this country what it was.

Your uncle, who lived downstairs, played the
mandolin and sang, and your mother—divorced
from your father—made herself beautiful
before going out.

I would walk up the street, calling your name
D - O - M - I - N - I - C   G - A - L - A - T - I
that had a melody I liked, wanting only a song,
and then we would play and tease each other,
and talk about our imaginary exploits,
big shots on the make, our imaginations
ricocheting over a world that was yet to come.

Horlick's Athletic field
for Ulysses Doss

Our most famous athletic field—
if famous it was—was, like our high school,
named after the Horlicks,
whose plant made the malted milk tablets
that *were* famous
or at least known to the world outside—

unlike Horlick Athletic Field
that was famous only to us
because Jackie Robinson once played there
before he reached the majors
and hit a home run, thrilling the fans forever,
an event that became a permanent part
of our tenuous myth and lore—

but if I missed that event (being too young)—
and much of the talk that followed—
I didn't miss the Racine Belles, of the
All-Girls Professional Baseball League,
with their short-skirted canary yellow uniforms
beneath the baseball caps
they bobby-pinned into place—

thrilling us and distracting us from
the concerns of the war
because for us they were more
than just a distraction, or morale booster,
they were ours and belonged to us,

and when I looked out from the stands
there—as irreplaceable as the sun,
and as golden, stood Clara Schillace,
the pig-tailed, olive-skinned centerfielder
with whom I was in love, and with whom
I stayed in love all the years
they played on that field,
when I was youth-wounded
and the world unstrung.

Poem

We sat the benches
on Monument Square
beside the shallow twin pools
of goldfish and lily pads,
with the statue between.

Its uncommon artful splendor
giving us pride in our simple
Midwestern town.

The Hunters

We hunted Scout's Woods by
first entering that open field
at the edge of town
where we encountered
the one same apple tree
waiting at the entrance
of the woods,
and there, just before we
loaded up, we stopped beside
that tree and threw branches
and bruised apples, until
each of us had at least one
good apple to eat. Horny,
hard, green, but tasty to us,
because we were standing
on the threshold of that
other space,
where everything would
be instantly transformed, bearing
no resemblance to our ordinary lives,
for we were about to enter
again our dream bodies, that would
connect us to powers we could feel
but not understand, there in that
twilight zone where boys become men.

Each time anew, that abused and abandoned
apple tree initiated us into that realm.

Lake Michigan

Although Racine (which meant Root in French) came to its location because of the river, it was, nevertheless, the river in conjunction with the lake that made it a valuable and viable setting.

But first the river had to be dredged and cleaned of its roots.

Later, piers were put in to break the waves, with a foghorn at the end of the north pier, and then, further out, a lighthouse station, that was called Reef Light.

The true lighthouse was located at the furthest northern reach of the territory that we thought of as *our place*—outside of the city proper, perhaps, but part of the city of our mind.

There was a pier just south of the lighthouse, a golf course above it, and in the parking lot that served the golf course and picnic grounds, we sometimes parked at night with our teenage dates and watched the "submarine races."

Beyond the lighthouse was no-man's land, but if you took the highway north from there you would eventually reach Milwaukee, where the lake would again come into view.

The Danes, who comprised nearly one-third of our population of 70,000, lived on the West Side, and everyone else lived either north or south. There was no east side. It belonged to the lake.

If a stranger asked where east was, we would answer, "That way, till your hat floats."

One winter, before I was born, it was so cold the lake froze solid for as far as one could see, and people walked all the way out to the Reef Light.

The lake lay below the city. Not far below, but just enough below that unless you were there, on the shore, or on one of its many piers, you were looking down at it. This we enjoyed doing, either from out our car windows, as we drove along the streets that bordered the lake, or looking down from the grassy knolls, or from the gazebo at North Beach, with its bathhouse and sandy expanse, that extended all the way to the zoo, a full mile away. Along that stretch of land, on the bluff above the lake, there were permanent benches, where the elderly and the thoughtful sat in quiet, looking out over the shifting colors of the lake.

Sailboats, rowboats, tugs, coalboats and barges traveled the lake and the river. And on the piers, early morning fishermen, who had obtained their bait from one of the many garages that lined the streets that led to the pier, where minnow and crab tanks were housed, with the craggy, unsmiling attendant, shuffling from house to garage at all hours, answering immediately the buzzer inside or outside the garage door, placed there for his customers.

Cooks' Shanty was the name of the whitewashed shed at the foot of North Pier. It was just big enough for Old Man Cook to turn around in once, with enough lateral space for perhaps two tiny steps both right and left. He sold minnows, candy bars, soda pop, potato chips, and rented poles for $1.00 each, 90 cents of which was the deposit.

Histories

What do we gain from our parents
that was never ours
but in being theirs was ours.
I wonder about the food and music
and especially the tongue
that never ceased to make me laugh or weep—
because I realize now that our tongue
has always been a member of the heart,
not the head;
a language for histories and passions,
spent, perhaps, but alive
alive always in the body of each man.

I put all that aside because so many
others could say it as well—
and take one thing, one thing alone
that is mine, that no one else can touch
or want to understand:
my father at an Armenian picnic, dancing,
round and round and round,
his whirling arms in a speech I could not
understand
with a knife tightly clenched in his teeth
held fast forever
in his bald and spinning head.

Ray Rodriguez

In a place and time when everyone
in our large community home
moved easily and casually
inside each other's homes and yards,
your family managed to separate
itself from us,
while maintaining their home
as a shelter against the world.

At least that was how it appeared
to me then.
Of all my friends homes, yours was
the only one I never entered.
But every day I went to school
I crossed the lot beside where you lived,
there on La Salle Street,
the same block that held the homes of
the Giragosians, Hansens, Sahagians, Hermes,
Sells, Fredericksens, Gengozians, and Flanigans,
among others, and where I spent all the time
that I didn't spend on my own block.

Yours was a family of great dignity
and pride, I knew,
and I couldn't help but feel that
you were hiding yourselves from us
either out of fear,
or because you couldn't share with us
what was different in you.

Was it because you were Mexicans?
Did you therefore feel scorned?
I couldn't and didn't believe that
that was the case.
I decided, finally, it was because
your parents were shy and private
and wished to be alone with their foreignness,
that it had never occurred to the rest of us
was a thing possible to hide.

We were in the same homeroom in junior high,
and our team took on all comers at football
during the recess hours.
You passed, I caught, and no one else
on that lot did either of these things
better than us.
We were never beaten, that I can remember.
We became good friends after that.
You didn't play team sports in high school,
and neither did I,
opting instead for my share of glory
in the world at large.

I never saw you again,
but for the time I returned
for my first reading in Racine,
a major event in my life,
for I felt like a homecoming hero,
whether I was or not.
Somehow, I heard you refused to
believe it was true—that I was

a poet, returning to read
in the sacred halls of the university.
I can see you still, standing
by the rear door of the darkened hall,
refusing to walk in, disbelieving,
but somehow, in spite of yourself,
believing, too.
When I looked up again
the door had closed and you were gone.

Dear Mrs. McKinney of the Sixth Grade

Hands down, you were my favorite
teacher at Garfield elementary,
or at any school since:
your stern, austere face, that
held an objective judgment of
everything in charge;
the patient way you taught,
out of a deep belief and respect
for learning,
and the good books you chose
to read aloud—in particular, Mark Twain;
and the punishment you handed
out (a twin cheek twist, just
once, with forefingers and thumbs)
embarrassed us only because
we had failed ourselves,
for we had wisely learned from you
the need for discipline and regard.

Long after I left that place
I saw you once waiting for a bus,
and though I returned your warm
smile, I hurried on.
Why didn't I stop, as I could
see you wanted me to? I deeply
regretted it for weeks, and there
are moments when I remember it still.
And nothing, not poem, not time
not anything for which I might
stand proud, can erase that seeming

failure of feeling and regard on
my part.
I loved you, I really did, and I
wish now that in stopping and chatting
with you for a moment I could have
shown it to you then,
instead of now, in this poem,
in which only time and loss, not
you and I, are the subject to be held.

Itinerants

for Even "Junior" Rognerud

What of the stores that weren't
stationary, the services that
moved by foot & pedal & wagon.
Or pulled by man, or that were horse-
drawn. Also the pick-up truck.

Weren't these the businesses
closest to our hearts.
Because in our minds they
were not businesses at all
or even enterprises
but something quite other
that we couldn't quite define
except to give them the name
they were represented by—

Mr. Miller, the radio repairman,
who smoked a cigar as no one else
could, who came to our door
with his satchel of tools—

The rag & paper man on his
horse-drawn wagon,
his clipped, accented speech
flitting the air

The stranger on bicycle
with a contraption for sharpening
scissors and knives—

the house painter who gave us his life history
and for no extra charge.

And best of all the bicycle-propelled
ice cream wagon man with his musical bell
that our sharp ears were attuned to hear
from far blocks away.

And we felt—without needing to
make our claim—
that this was the way to do business
and the only way to be alive—
not realizing that these men were
at the low end of the totem pole
of economics, without power or prestige,
except for their influence over us,
feeding our souls ahead of our bodies.

And so I went on studying them from
my armchair in the streets
which was the seat of my pants,
by which I sailed through my coming years
negotiating all my God-given rights
over the tenure of that block.

William Miller

Bill Miller fixed radios, traveling from home to home from his apartment on the corner of La Salle and Hamilton Streets. I can see him still, walking by himself, groomed in a well-worn suit and tie, and with an inner, imperturbable calm.

For some reason he did little repairing in his own home. We would phone him (or somehow get a message to him in the days before we had a phone) and he would come in the evening and fix our radio. Why he came in the evenings I do not know, unless of course he had another, regular full-time job, like all the other men I knew, in one or another of the factories, that is. Nor did I know that he was "colored," as the blacks were called then. I only knew that he seemed different from the other men, and for this reason I was attracted to him.

I was not any more or less attracted to him once I learned that he was colored (mulatto actually, another term from that time), because this was merely a fact to be attached *onto* him, whereas what compelled me to notice him and to go on noticing him, with that first edge of wonder and admiration that comes when a mystery is encountered, was something else: his quality of quiet dignity and pride, that I was unable not to notice, for wherever I looked my eye always stopped and became attached to the non-commonplace, the thing that misfit the design. I did not put any great importance on the fact that I, too, was different, knowing still that I could never fit in myself. My subject of study, in the beginning at least, was not myself but others. I was simply watching and learning—indirectly and unconsciously.

Mr. Miller—for that was his name—smoked cigars. He smoked them in a way that I had never seen before. In that time and place, each person was known for something, and this "thing" often carried such importance that it became, for others at least, the person himself. It was therefore not surprising that he seemed legendary to me for the reason alone that he smoked his cigars with particular expertise.

But there was more to the matter of his personality and his influence on me than that, because in addition to smoking cigars professionally, Mr. Miller fixed radios.

One day I asked him about his cigar smoking. I wanted to know why I never once saw him re-light one of his cigars. He told me, in the soft-spoken way he had, that he was able to keep his cigar lit for over an hour at a time by knowing just when to puff on it, and just how hard to puff on it, depending on the moisture of the tobacco, the climate and temperature of the day, and of course depending on how far down the cigar had been smoked. I was amazed and couldn't take my eyes off of him. Or his cigar. I didn't know what enthralled me more, the feat, or the style with which it was accomplished.

But in the end the thing that seems to lie at the basis of my remembrance of Mr. Miller is his dignity and pride. I had all along assumed that these qualities were inherent in him, but it may have been that he acquired them through suffering, and out of a deep, personal need to make something in himself that could deter prejudice and discrimination. I do not know. If this was the case then it may have been—again unconsciously—why he served as a model for me, and why in fact I admired him as much as I did.

Our Fathers

What about the fathers of my friends?
Didn't they also make things difficult
for their sons? Garabed's father:
tall, gaunt, taciturn—were they not
all taciturn—who sat forever
in his mohair armchair, brooding
over his secret thoughts,
complaining if a draft entered the room.
Did he suspect a Turkish invasion?

And why wasn't I aware of the large
broad-brimmed hat he wore,
that Art Bronaugh told me years later
set him apart as someone to notice
with wonder and awe.

Imagine, one of our fathers soliciting
that kind of response.
All I knew is what Garabed told me himself,
that he had asked his father to loosen up
and welcome his friends into their
home, and not embarrass him with
his gruff manner and detached aloofness,
because that is what his friends seemed to see
and nothing else.

And no telling what else Garabed or his brother
Kevork saw, or Rose, their young sister.
I mean, what about the other Armenian fathers,

weren't they just like my own,
filling the American landscape with their old
country ways, making us yearn desperately
for what we imagined the "American" kids
we chummed with had,
so certain that what they had was better
than what was ours.

Little did we know then about abuse, dysfunction,
psychosis, and the rest, since we were
only barely aware that we were loved, really loved,
and so we had to wait for it all to shake down
before we knew that those strange,
embarrassing, totally out of it fathers of ours
had given us something that couldn't be exchanged
for the most expensive coin minted
in this tarnished land of ours.

Yellow Bricks
for Ron Gardina

I didn't know that the color of the bricks
were the result of the clay soil
they were produced from,
because in my mind their tarnished
color—in appearance, dirty yellow-brown—
was the result of age, grime, neglect and
abuse, speaking of something deep inside
that was bound inextricably with my
own feelings of inferiority—the son
of immigrants, an only child, with afflictions
brought over from the Massacres
that I could not understand
but that our dead-end block reflected
in some way, as did that yellow brick
abandoned factory across the street,
taking up so much of that block,
and the punched out windows, targeted
by our stones, until there was nothing left
to destroy, as if I, or we, could
overcome that color and factory,
that sat like a cancer upon our block,
growing increasingly oppressive
as I grew increasingly upward
and outward, to a life that called
to me from beyond those walls.

Stu Faber

It takes forever to learn what our life
 means, going over the evidence spilled
 across the years, coming to conclusions
 based on the feelings the discovered facts
 reveal—so how can we know for another,
 how can we know what our influence has been
Certainly I never dreamed that my father was
 someone one of my friends would or could
 look up to and admire and would wish to
 win the respect of, or be grateful to for
 his kindness and regard
But Stu Faber, the son of our family doctor,
 who was not, ironically, at home in his
 body, clumsy at things the rest of us did
 without conscious thought, but who in turn
 did things none of the rest of us dreamed of:
 a disk jockey with his own radio program
 while still in high school, when he also
 had his own band
But we were friends for a time, long before we
 could have known that he would become
 a lawyer, and I an artist, something that
 would have been strange even to contemplate
 at the time, in those years when
I took him hunting when no one else would,
 calling him Elmer Fudd, while trying to teach
 him to shoot, which was a hopeless affair,
 but that he now remembers well, while I
 hardly remember it at all, and keeps the

name Elmer, still trying to belong, teaching
    himself the things I had long ago left behind
    as we both had the town and those childhood
    influences, or so we thought
Now meeting as adults, when I am told all of this,
    what I had forgotten—that he remembers
    with emotion—and the event in all of this
    that touched him most deeply was the rabbit
    I shot with him and brought home, that he
    watched me dress, and that Father invited
    him to share with us the following weekend
Which became one of the most important childhood
    experiences of his life, because on that day we made
    him a part of our family, as is natural with Armenians,
    and that was what he longed for: the intimacy
    and warmth I always took for granted, while what I
    had always wanted was what he had
With a father, unlike mine, who was not an immigrant,
    and unlike mine was a professional, and again unlike
    mine, was rich and lived with his family on the North
    Side, where I longed to be and belong
But unlike me, Stu did not grow up feeling he was
    loved by his father, and so he began to look
    outside his own environment for what he needed,
    not valuing anything he had that in his mind
    set him apart as privileged, and that embarrassed
    him, as the conditions of my background had shamed me
And then on that Sunday he found what he was looking
    for with us, and credited you, and was grateful to you,
    and it was me he admired, for having the father I had.

Charles Kamakian

When we thought of him we thought of his big nose. Not that he was tall, had large feet, a broad forehead, wiry hair, powerful hands, with quick staccato movements—but that he had a big nose.

Each person had a chief, identifying feature, and this was what he was known by, even though it was seldom mentioned. Although, being young, cruel, heartless and dumb, it was—it was very often mentioned.

Perhaps it was simply our astonishment, our own way of cataloging the unusual in order to make a fitting, composite and reasonable picture of life—even though, as we all knew, life was not reasonable, even if we quakingly hoped it might turn out to be intelligible once we grew up.

In the meantime, there were the streets, and the forms that moved about in the streets, and of that tribe we too were numbered.

Also we had names.

This is how we responded intelligently to our astonishment.

For as long as anyone could remember, Chuck Kamakian was called Horse. I believe it was Eggs Kirkorian or Kush Kashian who gave him that name, but then who gave them their names?

It didn't matter. It was the named, not the namer, that was important.

It would be another thirty years or more before I realized that Horse—or Chuck, or Charley, or Raz—was handsome, and had a host of qualities and features I was only subliminally aware of at the time. Least of which was his nose, although his nose was also fitting, and—after all, worthy of mention—and not at all big for his general size, and did, if anything, benefit, not distract, from his handsomeness, however much it might have once undermined his pride.

Nancy Jacobsen

I took you to the 9th grade prom.
We were a foursome: you and your
sister, and Lotch and me.

You lived on the far north side.
What we aspired to, from out of
the ghetto we didn't know then

was our home. You were bright,
blond, and beautiful. And very
far away. I don't know to this

day how we got to your place.
I only know how we got back.
In your father's car. We arrived

at your door, corsages in hand.
I was wearing a brand new suit,
my first, with the pockets still

sewn in place. No one at home
knew to cut them free. Was this
the tailor's proof that the suit

was new? Like leaving the tail on
the skinned coon, so the buyer
would know it wasn't cat? It all

went very fast, the getting there,
the dancing, all but the getting
back. Your father picked us up

because there was presumably,
no other way to get the two of
you home. Lotch got out with me

explaining that he lived just up
the hill and could easily walk.
You and your sis were angry with

your dad. It showed. And we were
embarrassed and frustrated. All we
wanted, the four of us, was to have

it end privately, secretly, and finally
separately. That we could have the
kiss that would seal the evening

so we could treasure what we didn't
know then was an experience that
would never come again. Your father

was as confused and discombobulated
as we were, trying to do the right thing,
and not knowing how. It was his first

prom, too, and sending his starry-eyed
daughters off with two dark strangers
from the other side of town must have

been as troubling for him as it was
discomfiting for us: who had ventured
so far from home. For the first time.

But it would not be the last.

Our Library

Built by Carnegie to fit our city's needs,
it stood there—as it does today—a solid,
square, yellow brick, two story building on the
corner of 7th and Main, just one block up
from Monument Square, and within sight of that
great lake, that I never failed to look out
upon each time I visited that place.

I went there first with my mother to the story
hour Saturday afternoons, and then for books to
take home, until I was old enough to have my own
card, searching the shelves with my growing needs,
fascinated by the hushed silence of the place,
the circular stairs that took me to areas I browsed,
standing on the thick glass floors I marveled at.

Downstairs there were books for older readers,
along with the newspaper and magazine racks,
beside the table where so many sat, who were there
to escape the elements and to find in the
journals and dailies some hope for their lives, or,
barring that, an excuse for their presence in that holy
atmosphere, beyond the wind and rain and cold of day.

My library card was free and it would never date,
for it was as renewable as my need. It was second in
importance only to the streets, where my first education
took place, that I would finally give shape and form to
because of the learning and knowledge I found within those
walls, where the spirit was aided to weld body to mind
from a grace that only the printed word could provide.

Thompsondale

We will never leave the picnic
    at Thompsondale
    our mothers ever beautiful
    in their summer dresses
Our fathers with straw hats
    and colored suspenders
A blanket spread upon the meadow
    cane poles strung
    with bobbers dancing over
    the slow moving stream

The grapeleaves gathered
    in the basket
    will never be taken home
    the sandwiches will be eaten
    again and again
And clouds will gather and part
    the sun will rise and recede
    night will come
And then tomorrow again and again

The Runaway

I began running away from home sometime after the age of ten.

I would walk up State Street after dusk, and stop, as a rule, at the pool hall and cigar store around the corner on Main Street. I might watch the pool players for awhile—or, if the owner threw me out, browse among the comics or paperback novels, whose covers contained barefooted Southern women, whose pretty faces were held up to the reader in a provocative pout or leer.

And then I would go home.

After a few years I began to notice the pattern. Even before I left the house I knew I would be returning home—well before morning.

But I couldn't give up *wanting* to run away, nor could I overcome the particular feeling of hurt that caused this compulsion in me to flee from home.

It only happened when I was hurt in a particular way. It occurred when I felt that something private in me had been outraged. It had to do with my true self not being understood, which caused me to feel violated.

My poor soul sensed its true state of homelessness and wanted to flee.

And then one day I realized that this life that seemed to have been thrust upon me could not be exchanged for another, truer life. What I needed had to be made. By me. And the time for that making had not arrived.

Below

The city's smallest park
there behind the
downtown theaters
and below the street
that followed the lake

With a bench or two
a patch of grass
and a view of blue water
clear to the horizon

I had come from the busy city
to sit on the grass alone
absorbed in the life
of that place
that for the moment
was home

Pigeons

We saw the pigeons
    among the silos
    when we drove
    the country lanes
Feeding on the fallen corn
    of harvested fields
    gliding the air
    self-propelled
Like our balsam planes
    but never crashing
    or coming up lame
To whom did they belong
    there in the leaf-torn trees
    among the
    habitations of man

Then

when barefooted on the hot earth
we moved along to the river's quiet shore

bucket in one arm with a can of worms
poles over our shoulders & whistling a tune

men would stop and question
and ask us where we went

and now I know what caused their longing
now that that part of my life is spent

The Bridge

The State Street bridge would be my bridge for many years to come. It was the bridge I would cross most often, on my way to the Mainstreet Theatre and the movie houses beyond: Badger, Venetian, Rialto, as well as the pool hall below Ace Grill, the pinball machines at the Arcade, Luby's Bowling Alley, where I later set pins, and of course for shopping, especially in the fall, before the start of the new school year.

Later there would be other bridges.

At the bottom of Liberty Street, the Island Park bridge, as well as the one at the end of Sixth Street, its other entrance—that I only discovered years later. Another, the Main Street bridge, could almost be seen from the State Street bridge, and was the last Root River bridge before the river emptied into the lake.

These were the main bridges—the city bridges—the ones I would have to cross and recross as I went out from home and began to experience the life of the city.

I would later discover other bridges, in the city and out of the city, as I moved through my days, following the life of people and the life of water. One took me to the outer events that nourished my thirst for the meaning of life, and the other, the life of water, brought me to inner events, and carried me to deeper and deeper streams within myself.

The bridges I traveled over carried me to both.

III

10 Years Later

Standing on the leafy bank
on my first day back
overlooking hills & ravines
and the river I fished,
I knelt, reached back over
the years, and threw a stick
that tumbled a wild green apple.

One bite and it all came back.

I didn't want to protect myself

I didn't want to protect myself
by seeking perfection against the
accidental onslaughts of time—
but instead to move imperfectly
through it all, not to be the best
or the only, or the one to watch,
but rather the beggar of mercy
and grace, finding new hope
in each disappointment,
believing against reason
(against what the senses said
could not be) that there
was an order beyond this
disorder, that there was
a truth beyond this lie:
and that I was included
in its design,
that could not be seen
or named
but could be believed in,
if one believed that one
was loved.

Island Park

Following the freedom of that river
I came to the pavilion in the park.
An only light was there. I was in the
dark. In the circle of that halo a city
danced. But I was not there. I was
by the river that held me in its
lonely breath. Behind me, night sounds
of frogs and crickets. And silent
animals crouched in the grass. I waited
a long minute, the light before me,
the dark behind, and turning round
I made my first small choice for this
other, separate life.

The Peasant

You walked with bare
peasant feet
from garden to kitchen
and back again,
confusing me, making
me wonder what others
would think, in your
BVDs, unashamed
of your body,
at home with your flesh

before you began tiring slowly
from a lifetime of enduring,
old when I first saw you even,
and certainly by the time I
recognized you as father

and half of what you were is what
I am, whether pushing it
with pride, or momentarily
concealing it to reveal
or make known the other side

but your side, the peasant side,
is always there, with me,
unafraid, silent, present,
the ground I stand on,
move and turn in, to face
the other ways not seen
by you or needed by you,
but that do not make me
any less your son.

Armenian Coffee Houses in America

Armenian coffee houses in America
resemble without difficulty
those of the old country.
The inhabitants are the same,
desiring Turkish coffee and
cards or backgammon. But in
America they also share a
loneliness for Armenia and a
need for old country traditions.

But one by one they are closing down.
Of course who can blame the owners:
the old men are kicking off and
their sons have little interest
in the Armenian way of life.

Jezvehs and demitasse cups are kept
in the pantry. Occasionally an honored
guest is served in the traditional
manner, or a curious friend interested
in Oriental customs.

Willie

Willie, the time comes round again
to remember your wagon of junk.

Whenever my mind moves up Douglas
Avenue, it stops at La Salle Street

And sees us all again,
coming and going

That idiot smile on your face—
you too a child like us.

You invited us to know you then,
but we only teased and ran.

We are all lost, you are now dead;
your measure has become an innocence
I keep under my bed.

Kewpees

Years before the fast food boom
took over the country
we had such an eatery in Racine,
that was known not for being fast,
but for being good,
and not just because it was convenient,
but for being familiar. And reliable.
The same service. The same food
and atmosphere—every time!

Kewpees sole food, in my mind,
was hamburgers.
They also served pies & cakes
but I can't recall ever having ordered
either of these.
Only hamburgers (usually two)
which were always cooked the same way,
wrapped in the familiar paper covering
with the Kewpee doll printed in blue,
and the lettered slogan: *we cater to all the folks*

There was no waiting because the ground beef
was always cooked and ready,
pushed to the back of the flat top burner
from where it was scooped
into the familiar hamburger bun.
With a pickle placed on top.
Then wrapped and served to its customers.

Most everyone sat at the counter
but there were tables for larger parties.

Root beer was the drink of choice,
and I don't believe anyone tipped,
since the service was minimal,
with the napkin holder on the counter,
the paper wrapper our plate,
and the service so swift,
the eating so quickly accomplished

That you were in and out in an experience
bordering at once on tradition and ritual,
since it seemed to be the one place,
the one event, the one experience,
we all shared in common,
because downtown was where we shopped
and Kewpees was where we ate.

The Friday Night Fish Fry

If we didn't go bar-hopping or to
the movies with our buddies,
we went—once old enough—

to one of the many bars
for the Friday Nite Fish Fry,
a tradition in our city because of

Lake Michigan and its famous perch.
For Friday was payday, the day the
eagle shat, squatting where he perched

the remainder of the week (on the
J. I. Case globe), looking down over
that land we called ours.

The Trains

We took the trains for granted—
their coming and going, their hooting
and whistling, the sounds so different
in daylight than at night—because at each
age and period of our life they sent
a different signal to the transmitting
apparatus that was the stationmaster inside
our minds and hearts.

The depot was also a place of comfort and retreat.
A place where no one would be bothered,
where you bought a ticket or didn't, where you went
to leave, or stayed to await someone who was
arriving from a place they had left behind.
Or it might be someone returning home
after long absence, the war: servicemen
in uniforms, business men in suits,
or distant uncles and aunts.

It was good to have a railroad depot,
where people arrived with news
that was foreign and strange, or departed
to seek whatever it was they could not find in their own
home place.

It was the Northwestern Railroad Station for us,
that divided north from south in our town,
but that didn't belong to either location,
serving the city with dispassionate regard,
strangely singular, in possession of nothing

of its own, but allowing a barter
on the future, or a payment on the day,
with an odor that was uniquely its own,
sanctifying nothing but itself.

Father's Turk

After the war, when you became
an American citizen, were you glad
that you didn't kill the Turk that you
were told was in your company—
for no reason but that he was there—
claiming that imprisonment would
not have troubled you, for it would have
been worth it after what they had done
to you and all our people.

Years went by, I was born, you died,
and the stories about you that could
have been told were buried
with you, making it so hard for me
to wander with you over your life,
that I felt I needed to do in order
to better inhabit my own.
For am I not also you, and are you
not also me, torn away not only by
time but by my own neglect.
I wanted just once to sit with you
and listen to Shah-Mouradian sing,
the great Armenian hero whose voice
bled for the suffering of our nation

Who came to Racine once and sang
at Dania Hall, there beside the Hotel
Thomas where you once worked.
I sat in the balcony years later, after
you were gone and imagined it,
imagining it without you, as I have had
to imagine so many things we might have shared.

Abby

Next door to Garfield Elementary
just above the playground, lived
the Mikaelian family. Abby, the
third son, stood alone on their lawn
and roared at the top of his lungs.
It was not an hysterical or angry
cry, just a bellow, loud and strong
and clear, and though it may have
had an intentional meaning, being
a specific call to someone or other,
what it meant to me, simply, was one
brave man calling out his anonymous
name to the unresponding universe.

It was a call I relished, because here
was someone, half mad, I thought, but
with a joyous inner freedom, reveling
in his own humanity—vulnerable, unsecured,
but fearless and undaunted. He was
for me the first Armenian to punctuate
the American landscape with a signature
that was his alone. Some day, one way
or another, I would add my name to that.

1950

It must have been 1950. Racine, Wisconsin.
I was nineteen, my father sixty
or sixty one—
It must have been my first car, a Plymouth.
My father never drove, nor my mother.
Only one Armenian family,
as I remember, owned a car back then.

It is evening and I am driving him
to the Veterans building for some event
or meeting that he is attending.
We are downtown before I realize that
he is uncertain of the address.
He is used to walking everywhere,
and has become disoriented in my car
(but I don't realize any of this
at the time). I am being impatient
with him. I don't like being his chauffeur,
I want to get on my with my life, not
be a helpmate in his.

Pull over, he says, reading my thoughts.
Which I do, feeling a little
uneasy, my conscience fighting
with my impatience. But I
pull over. He gets out and quickly
begins his hurried walk—
the walk I will always know
him by, and that I will always remember
when I think of him and think of myself.

He gets out in front of Woolworth's.
It is dark out, but the street lights
are not on, and I am there, alone
in the semi-darkness,
unable to move, my car stationed at the curb.

And I am there still, watching,
staring at his back as he moves away,
knowing the Veterans building
is just three blocks away.
I would call if he could hear me
but he is on his own and alone
as I am
with whatever this is that I am.

Father's America

There is a photograph of you
sitting on an overturned bucket
in Zaehler's backyard,
with Bill and a relative
in the background,
and there is this sense that
though you are an outsider
you have been included
in this gathering of hearty, ·
garrulous men, whose lives
are so different from yours:
part-time fishermen, men with
guns and nets, and junk autos
that they drive and fix—
embodiments, fixtures, of the American
scene—and yet there you are,
no different really than what
I recognize myself to be—one who
could be and might be included
but who stands separated
by temperament, history, and
a sensibility that I have come to
examine microscopically,
perhaps for us both:
for you were an Armenian in America,
whereas I was an American inside
an Armenia I never saw or longed for,
except for the tracings, the lines
of affinity the blood makes,
that will not leave us alone.

Gob Kaiserlian

Although you were older than me,
you were, of all the Kaiserlians—
who were my role models then—
the most artistic, the greatest dreamer,
and the person I felt the deepest
affinity with.

I never understood why you didn't believe
in yourself, for even as a boy I knew
you would eventually be overcome
by your own posture of defeat.
What was it in you that understood
the beautiful, without believing the
beautiful would ever enter your life?
And what more did you need to wish for
than that separate life you dreamed
for others could also be possible
for you, if you had fought for it,
as you knew you must.

When Ardie and Mikey and I were working
with crayons on our coloring books,
you were drawing in pastels,
making still lives that dazzled me—
in particular the one that featured
an eggplant, its luminous purple
and sensual contours
lighting the room your mother hung it in.
I never visited your home without
noticing it—often studying it—

convinced you had the talent
to which I only aspired.

Your ironic sense of humor
bordered on the black, especially
when you turned it against yourself.
Mohr-Jones became More Junk,
Sears-Roebuck, Sear's Rubbish,
and the logo you suggested for J. I. Case
(where you ground down your own days),
was a crushed avocado.
You only went to two baseball games
in your life, and the time between them
was twenty years, but you noticed and pointed out
that one of the outfielders was still
in the position you had left him in.
Stan Musial. You were right.
You somehow escaped the futile, dead-end—
and yet wondrous—fascination the rest
of us had with sports.

Once, long before I owned a car
or a proper suit of clothes,
we drove together to Milwaukee
to a supper club—my first—
and listened to the Red Norvo Trio,
with Tal Farlow on the guitar.
I ate squab—another first—
and knew, while I was experiencing it,
that I was having one of the timeless
moments of my life.

Your favorite song was "Summertime."
I cannot hear it without thinking of you,
and listening to the lyrics
I understand why.

Father

He did not once say, I miss my home
    I want to return
    nor did I once reveal
    that I felt hurt for him, or
    for myself
Our sorrow was too great for that
    his repressed
    my own still unrevealed

And was my melancholy an imitation of his
    and my temper as well
Did we want to understand ourselves
    or the other—and could we have

What can one man know of another's grief
    especially when that one is still a boy
    and the other had been boyhood robbed

I stand vigil in the silence
    of the eternity you disappeared into
    knowing above all
    that I did not know you
    and that it would have been
    an intrusion to have tried

Our private lives are all we ever had
    and also what we shared and share now
    because the caring that went into living
    does not stop with your death
    nor will it end with mine.

Dafje Vartan

Dafje dafje, tambourine man,
who came to our weddings and
played and sang—oud and dumbeg,
a three man band.

All the way from South Milwaukee
and back again.

(So much for legend, memory and song,
men and instruments all long gone).

Dafje dafje, this one last song

The Lake

One drove there always
    when going north or
    south of east
    following the lake
    that was like a sea
The homes on its banks
    palatial
    or stylishly modern
    the older city little
    resembling what the rest
    had become
No longer the Belle City on the Lake
    without rival or peer
    but this heterogeneous settlement
    of people from every economic sphere

Alone in one's car
    driving along the way
    the imagination wandered
    over distant landscapes
    and also one's own
And for once—and for as long
    as we drove—
We felt limitless,
    tranquil,
    and at peace,
    with possibilities ahead
    whether on these shores or another

For the calm of the lake was in us
        the peace in the landscape was ours
        and carried us to possibilities
        we knew we would one day explore

Going

Unloading boxcars
on Erie Street
for quick money

taking anything
that came along
always on the run

which was anywhere
and going
because I never

stood still
and sold siding, shoes,
awnings, pots & pans

you name it
whatever came
around the block

I jumped and rode it
until I got bucked
or bored

waiting for that one train
the great chance
to ride the rattling rails

down that U. S. track
in the boxcar that
held my name

or anyhow
that's what I thought
I was waiting on
until it came and I went

Father's Time

I make the picture
you enter
as you move

down State Street,
intersecting your humanity
from the past

while you put on your jacket
then leave your work
at the hotel bar & grill

to enter Main Street
while I walk up State
both streets different now

except perhaps where
they meet
at the Mainstreet Theatre

the billboard in back
ever there & changing
that I now have to turn

and look back at to see
there the coming events
anticipating the days before

wondering over your time
where you have gone
and what you are coming to

the Army yet beyond
your bride-to-be lost on the death
march in the desert

that she alone of her family will
survive, as you will the war in France,
but by now you have reached

the State Street bridge that
I would stand upon
year after year

looking down its turgid waters
the wheeling gulls overhead
the lights coming up

from the darkened surface
a lone boatman and strangers
in the street

but you are unseen and alone
pausing to finger the green
surface of that latticed rail

seeing your life or forgetting it
beside me
invisibly there

and in that moment
I touch your eternity
and we disappear

Beside the River

BOOK ONE

Garfield School

I was staring out the window at the playground below. It was deserted, where just moments before we had all been shouting and playing. Now we were cooped up in our classroom, which for me was a prison. It was a prison for all of us who felt unwanted. Not just the other Armenian kids like me, but anyone whose parents were foreign, or any of those who thought of themselves as something other than American. Like the Jews, Greeks, and Italians, for instance. We envied the Americans—as everyone else excepting the blacks was called—and we would have liked to be Americans ourselves, but not if it meant giving up whatever else we were.

I was listening to the clanking of milk bottles and garbage cans. I looked out the window again. Our playground was backed by the buildings on State Street. The raised voices of the women in the tenements carried across the yard. We were on the same level, but they were far enough away that I couldn't hear their talk. One of them was shaking out her mop and talking to her neighbor, who was hanging clothes on the line. She turned now and leaned on her mop and stared up at the sky. I wondered what was going through her mind.

"Steven," Miss Ransard called. I turned and looked at her, even though my name isn't Steven. My name is Stepan Bakaian, or Step for short. I've been called Bak also, which isn't as cool, but it's better than Steven, which is my "American" name, given to me in the first grade by that old battle-axe Swanson. That's the grade when all the foreign kids got their American names.

I looked down at my copy of the Fifth Reader, which Miss Ransard was holding open in front of her. She was staring at me over the top of the cracked spine, her bifocals about to slide off her delicate nose. "Yes," I said grudgingly.

"*Well,*" she said, dragging out the word until the room filled with her voice as well as with her impatience and contempt for me. "We were reading about how the barbarians stormed the gates of China and nearly toppled an empire, and how, as a result, they caused the erection of the Great Wall of China, one of the monumental achievements of Man. Don't you care about what Man has *done*? Don't you find this *fascinating*?"

I stared back at her, but I didn't answer the statement she pretended was a question. I was thinking to myself that the only thing fascinating about what she had said was that it was the first time I could remember any of my teachers mentioning the Chinese. All we ever got was American history and European history. I don't think there was one word in any of the books we were taught from about the Armenians. All the Americans ever said about us was that we were the starving Armenians, which in their minds was anything but fascinating. They talked about us as if we didn't really exist—like we were so far away in their minds that we were nowhere at all. Well, those starving Armenians happened to be my relatives. My own aunt was one of them, or she would have been my aunt if she hadn't starved to death before I was born. That was my father's sister. But it was even worse for my mom. She lost everybody, and not just from starvation alone, but from cholera, dysentery, and outright murder. That was during World War One, when the Turks tried to get rid of all the Armenians living in their country.

I wanted to tell her to take the Chinese wall and shove it. But I didn't. I had already flunked the second grade once and the fifth grade twice—once during the regular year, and again at the summer session. Grade school had become a jail sentence, and all I wanted was to get through it and move on to junior high, where it might be different.

I looked from Miss Ransard to the clock on the wall, considering what to say. I couldn't help but notice that I was being stared at by everyone in the room. Some of my classmates were looking at me with pity and others with scorn, but the Armenian kids only looked embarrassed.

The bell rang in the hallway, announcing the end of class. "All right, children," Miss Ransard said, "put your books away neatly, stand up, and file out. We're going across the hall to Room Ten for your first music lesson with Miss Schultz. Be alert and attentive, now. Make me proud of you."

Root River

I had taken my bike out of the rack and I was absent mindedly bouncing the front tire up and down on the pavement, while cursing Miss Ransard under my breath. Several boys were circling the large elm tree in the school yard and calling out teasing remarks to the girls as they walked by. I turned my bike around and headed for the back gate.

I pretended to be invisible as I rode up State Street to Forest Street, and then down Liberty Street to Island Park. I didn't know where I was going and I didn't want to know. I circled the park twice. It was deserted except for two old men sitting on one of the benches above the winding river.

I was getting ready to cross back over the Liberty Street bridge and head for home, but I changed my mind at the last minute. Instead of dismounting, I rode up to the cement railing that came up to my waist and seated myself on the bridge while holding onto my bike with my feet. In the yard facing the park was a rock garden that imitated in miniature the bridge I was sitting on. I wondered who the man was that had made the rock garden. It had always fascinated me, and I had never walked across the bridge without stopping to look at it.

I lowered my eyes from the garden to the river below and

watched it turn out of my sight around the bend beyond the park on its way to Lake Michigan, where its brown waters would enter the life of the great blue lake.

I lowered myself onto my bike and headed up the hill, taking the back streets and alleys to my home. I entered our backyard by riding through our neighbor's yard, which was on the street behind ours. I parked my bike against the rear of our house, facing the garden and grape arbor built by the German family who lived here before we did. It wasn't something my father could have built.

My mom was in the kitchen preparing supper. I walked to the ice box and dished some yogurt into a saucer.

"Hello, *yavroos*," she said.

"Hello, Mom." I sprinkled some sugar over my yogurt and sat down at the table. I was watching my mother's fingertips as she spread out a grape leaf. She sprinkled some water on the filling before placing a portion of ground lamb and rice into the spread leaf, turning in the two ends, and rolling it into a perfect cylinder.

"You didn't come straight home," she said without looking up from her work. "In the Old Country it was horses, and in the new country it's bikes and autos. It is the same, yes? Men like to go out. They like to come home, but not before they've gone out. Your father came all the way to America—do you know why?" She paused without looking up from her work. "So he could go home again, buy a white horse, and ride over his newly purchased land, a *pasha*. You didn't know that."

"No," I said, "I didn't know that."

She wiped a hair from her forehead with her wrist and then dipped her fingers in the water glass before sprinkling the filling. "You see, you are not so different from your father."

"I'm an American."

"You are also an Armenian."

"Yes," I admitted, "an Armenian-American. That's what everyone tells me."

148

"You're grumbling again. Now what is it?"

"I'm one thing inside—myself—but on the outside I'm these two things, and I don't know what either one is supposed to be."

Mother stopped her work to look at me. "So what! Is it something terrible?" Are you being tortured? Have they taken your passport away?"

"What passport?" I shouted.

"Shut up and eat your yogurt."

"I don't have to shut up."

"Listen to me. I want you to be a proud Armenian. We are a great people with a great history. We were the first nation to adopt Christianity."

"Yeah, and before that we worshiped fire, right?"

She ignored the question. "We are older and wiser than the Americans. They have no common sense. Look how they live. Look how they raise their children—like chickens, any which way. If you want to know, that's how you are an American: you have no common sense."

"You and your common sense. If the Armenians had any common sense, they would have gotten out of Turkey and not gotten themselves slaughtered."

"That's finished. Now we are here. Our back is turned from that."

"What are you talking about? That's all any of you think about. Whenever there's an earthquake in Turkey, you rejoice. Our biggest heroes are martyrs. Our holidays celebrate battle scenes and death. Defeat, defeat, defeat—"

"We have hope. And our hope is you. Don't forget your *jeentz*. You are here. Fine! You're an American. That's good! I'm happy! But you come from somewhere else. You can have a great future—here in America. Your America. But you already have a great past—that was prepared for you in advance. We didn't suffer for nothing. We suffered for you. You're our hope!" She looked down at the grape leaf spread in front of her and quickly rolled it and placed it in the cooking pan.

"And what am I supposed to do in America?"

"It doesn't matter. Whatever you choose. First you will be educated, and then we will see. With your *jarbeek* you will change America."

"It takes more than genes and enterprise," I said. "How about pull, influence, and being in the right place at the right time with the right people? I don't see the Armenians putting on a show with their *jeentz* and their *jarbeek*."

"What show?" My mother looked up from her work and scowled at me. "This is not a contest on the radio. This is life, not a movie. You will see. One generation, two generations—we will make even America rich."

"Ma, for crying out loud, they don't even want us here."

"What are you saying? This is the land of promise, of hope. This country is our salvation. They took us in. They sheltered us. We have made a home here, a community, everything!"

"But we're not Americans."

"Thank God!"

"Ma, what are you saying?"

"We're American enough."

"Enough for you maybe, but not enough for me."

Nicky Tekeyan

Every time I had one of these discussions with my mom, I had to get out of the house in a hurry. I slammed the door to let her know how I felt. But instead of getting on my bike, I walked down the rickety stairs at the end of our dead-end block and headed for my friend Nicky's house. I walked up Prospect Street and turned the corner at La Salle. High above my head a redheaded woodpecker was hammering away at one of the trees I had just walked under. I got a glimpse of him, but when I moved around the tree to have a better look, he just circled ahead of me while climbing higher and higher in the tree. "Come back," I hollered, as if he could understand English. But he kept climbing higher. "*Yegour*," I said again, this time in Armenian, and he disappeared from sight.

I kicked a pebble along the ground, trying to see if I could keep it on the sidewalk, so it would be a game. It lasted for six squares before ricocheting into the grass. I hurried up the street looking down, hoping to find something usable, like a discarded pack of cigarettes so I could add to my tinfoil collection. When I came to the Tekeyans', I walked in the front door and peered into the living room. Lily was sitting by herself on the couch, listening to a Duke Ellington record. Eva was in the dining room, ironing, but Arpey, Avak, and Nicky were nowhere in sight. "Nicky's on the upstairs porch," Lilly said, "trying out his new airplane."

"Thanks," I said, and bounded up the stairs. When I opened the door to the porch, Nicky was winding the propeller on his latest model airplane. "Hi ya, Step," he said.

"Wait up," I called. "Let me have a look at your plane before you set it off. I don't want to miss out on the crash."

"Don't say that—you'll bring me bad luck. Not that anything could go wrong, of course."

"What do you mean?" I said. "You always crash them—sooner or later."

"It ain't inevitable, you know. It's just a matter of time before I perfect my technique and make one that will never crash."

"Fat chance," I said. "Even if nothing gets in its way, like that wall out there, you can't count on a perfect landing."

"That's what I'm working on. If the weight distribution is just right, it won't ever crash."

"Well, you've got a good day for it," I conceded. There weren't any kids playing in the empty lot next to Nicky's house, which I knew was the reason he was out flying.

"I'm not like you," Nicky said, "wanting to fly planes through the trees or setting them on fire before takeoff, hoping they'll burn up in midair and come crashing down in a trail of smoke, like in the movies. Not that you've built a plane since I can remember."

"I'm saving my money for better things," I said, "but I like watching you send yours off. Anyhow, I wish there was a way to figure out how to get the pilot out safely by parachute once the plane goes up in smoke. That would really be something."

"It won't ever happen. The genius who could figure out how to do that with a toy would put his energy into something constructive."

"Well, he wouldn't if he were twelve years old."

"Yea, but there aren't any twelve-year-old geniuses that I've heard of."

"How about sailing it through the trees?" I said. "Just to try your luck. Maybe it'll get through unscratched."

I figured with Nicky's luck he could make it. Maybe. But he wasn't into luck, he was into figuring out how things worked. Luck was a byproduct of his curiosity was how Lily explained it to me one day. Lily understood everything.

Nicky's plane was wound up and ready to go. "Okay, Buckeye," he said, "three and a half loops to a perfect landing. Go ahead and do your stuff." Old Buckeye made a loop and a dive, then arched into a long, sweeping flight that I was afraid would take it into the street. But it seemed to put on the brakes at the last second and came down just short of the sidewalk in front of the street.

"Perfection," Nicky hollered. "See that, Step? Isn't she a beaut!"

We raced down the steps and out the door. "Let's try her again," I said.

"Not today, Step. I want to revel in the glory of my ace here for at least twenty-four hours."

"See you tomorrow, then," I said and laughed, "Should I bring my matches?" But Nicky didn't even hear me. He was holding his plane up, shoulder high and in mock flight, while imitating the sound of a humming engine as he headed back across the lot.

Willy Springer

It was Friday afternoon—at last. The first week of school was over. I had come straight home from class and I was in my room sorting out my baseball cards when I heard Willy Springer's truck pull up outside. The Springers were our next-door neighbors. Willy worked in Chicago as a photoengraver. He was also a drummer for a pickup band that played for weddings and practiced every Wednesday night in their parlor. But best of all Willy was a fisherman who fished with nets—not like the ordinary fishermen who used cane poles. He seined Root River for bait, and he used nets on Lake Michigan to catch perch and herring and lake trout. I always dreamed that he would take me out on his boat one day, but so far I hadn't been asked. I was too proud to ask myself, or even hint that I wanted to go out with him.

When he pulled up in his truck, instead of his old jalopy, it meant that he had been to the lake. I could hear the raised voices from my room, including his nephews'. They lived the next street over.

I walked outside to our grape arbor, sat down, and waited for them to back the truck between our homes to their backyard, where they would begin hauling out the boxes loaded with their nets and their catch.

I could see my father through the grape leaves, barefoot as usual, hoeing among the weeds. All that was left of his summer crop were some tubers and a patch of Swiss chard that was nearly two and a half feet high and came up to his waist, from where I was sitting. He wanted my mom to use the Swiss chard for *Sarma*, but she refused, preferring the traditional grape leaves she was used to. He called to me to come and have a look at his garden, but I didn't answer. He gestured again, pointing to the ground at something he wanted me to come and have a look at. I made a face and turned away.

Just then, Willy's son, Freddie, came bounding out of the house to join the men in the yard. They were poling the nets and throwing the squirming fish into boxes, dividing them by size. Willy's nephews, Frank and Bobby—my playmates—began cleaning the fish while the two men, Willy and his cousin Charley, worked at the nets. Freddie went down the basement stairs at the rear of their house and soon returned with a block of ice hoisted over his right shoulder by pincers, like the regular icemen used. With his ice pick in hand, he quickly began chipping pieces into one of the rectangular boxes. Frank and Bobby worked as a team. Frank grabbed one of the living perch, banged its head on the side of the boxboard, instantly scaled it, and then tossed it to Bobby, who slit the stomach open, and cutting off the head, slid the guts out in a piece. He tossed the cleaned fish into Freddie's box of ice.

Just as soon as Freddie had enough fish to fill an order, he covered the load with a gunnysack and went riding off to one of the taverns that had a standing order with the Springers. All of the taverns in Racine that had kitchens specialized in Friday night fish fries.

While all this was going on, Willy's scroungy cats were wailing for fish heads and guts. They kept edging closer, meowing plaintively. Bobby enjoyed peppering them with his fish heads. After jumping and screeching, they'd rush back in a pack and pounce on the dirt-covered heads and guts.

Willy's dog, Bozo, was racing madly about. The excitement of howling cats, working men, and jumping fish crashing against the boxes was driving him crazy. But no one, least of all the cats, paid any attention to him.

I was dying to walk over and have a look at the fish, especially the herring, because they were seldom caught off the pier, and also the trout, which could only be caught with nets, as they ran deep and never came near shore.

I had been sitting on the round table in the arbor, with my feet on the bench. I stood up now to have a better look, being careful not to be seen. If I couldn't be a part of something myself, I liked looking in on it without being noticed.

"Hey there, Sonny," Willie called out to me. He had spotted me without my noticing. "The perch are running. Yessiree Bob, running to beat the band. Ask the boys here."

Willy Springer called all the boys in the neighborhood Sonny and the girls Sis.

"You know what they say, 'When the wind's from the south, it blows the bait into the fish's mouth.'" He licked a finger and stuck it up in the air. "Sure enough!" he pronounced, laughing to himself and giving a wink and a clap, followed by a little bend and half step, which was his routine and trademark whenever he was feeling happy about something.

If I had thought about it, I would have known that what he was happy about was the catch they had made, the money he would soon be taking in, and—this being Friday night—the time he would have on the town with his wife, Matty. But I took the wink as being for me, for the running fish, and also for the sheer joy of fishing—in this case, *good* fishing—that he was letting me in on.

I jumped down from the bench, reached under the table for my pail, and then took a pole down from the rain spout below the slope of our roof.

"Goin' to the pier," I shouted to my mom through the kitchen window that looked out on our backyard.

"Take one of these perch for fish bait," Willy said. "You won't need anything else."

I shooed Bozo with my pole, without having any effect on his barking, and looked down at the wash bucket of breathing, squirming fish. Willy picked out a medium-sized perch and dropped it in my bucket.

Joe Perch

I hurried down the rickety stairs of our dead-end block on the street below, which led to the lake. Ours was the second to last house on the block, and the Springers' was the last. I always rode to Root River, but to Lake Michigan I walked—and not just because it was a lot closer than the river, but because there wasn't a safe place to park my bike near the pier, and I didn't want to invest in a tire guard. I had better things to spend my money on. Also, I liked to walk because of the factories near the lake that I would have to wind my way through, and where I sometimes found useful junk.

But an even better reason was the tiny park halfway between our house and the lake, which contained a tiny fountain. I always stopped there for a long drink of water. I liked the damp smell, and while I drank I'd stare past the perforated brass ball at the white and brown pebbles of stone.

From the factories I could hear the blast of the foghorn at the end of the pier. I hurried my step. I could see the masts of the sailboats. The smell of the lake was in my nostrils. As I passed the marina and headed up the pier, I cast my eyes down at the filthy brown water on the harbor side of the lake. It was polluted with condoms, bottles, and the refuse spewed up from the city sewers, as well as bloated fish. The contrast was startling, for the water on the other side of the pier was blue and clear and good enough to drink.

One of the thrills that went with fishing on the pier was stopping on the way out to watch Joe Perch, and also to admire his catch. He was the master fisherman of the pier and always had a stringer full of perch, whether or not the fish were biting for anyone else. The thing that made him different, right off, was that he fished close in, where the water was no more than five or six feet deep. The pier was shored up at this point with huge white boulders that were clearly visible.

The only thing Joe Perch had in common with the rest of us was that he used cane poles—not one or two, like us, but three. Except for his imitators, he was the only one on the pier to use bobbers, and not ordinary store-bought bobbers, but wine bottle corks fastened to his lines with matchsticks. Also, he didn't put any sinkers on his lines, nor did he ever switch bait, like we did—from crab tails to minnows to worms to fish bait and then back again. No, he fished exclusively with minnows, and not hooked through the back and head, but *under* the back and below the spine, so they would stay alive. He would ease them carefully into the water, and every now and then, when the waves churned against the rocks, you could see one of his minnows floating toward the surface, swimming gamefully.

"Hot dog," I shouted. I had stopped in front of Joe Perch and was staring down at his long stringer of fish. "Wowie, Joe, some fishing!" Joe Perch didn't bother to turn around. He was all business when it came to fishing.

I continued walking out to my spot at the end of the pier. I could see for myself that no one else was having any luck. Willy had tricked me again. The fish weren't biting.

I caught three small perch and quit. But I didn't really care, because about the time I was getting ready to quit I remembered it was Friday, and that meant payday. I could hear J. I. Case's whistle tooting in the distance, which meant the day shift was over. The logo for Case was an eagle, and the workers like to say that the eagle shits on Friday, which meant they would be getting paid.

And Friday night for me meant shoeshining with a friend, a chance to make some money of my own. So it was a kind of payday for me also.

"Never mind," my mother said when I walked into the kitchen with my embarrassing catch. "What did you expect?"

"How come I can't learn that the fish are never biting when Willy says they are?"

"Because you want to believe him. Also you know he isn't necessarily lying. Exaggerating maybe, but not lying. He wants you to catch fish, and he enjoys seeing you go off...."

"But why can't I learn my lesson?"

"Because you're a dreamer, like Willy. You hope they're biting instead of determining for yourself whether they are biting or not."

"No one can know that, Mom, for crumb's sake. The only way to find out is to go to the pier."

"Then what are you complaining about? You went—they weren't biting. Next time you go, they'll bite."

"No they won't."

"Shut up and wash your hands and face. Then you can eat. Your food is warming on the stove."

I walked past my dad, who was sitting in the dining room. He was smoking a cigarette and listening to the news on the radio. It was Gabriel Heater, shouting about the war. My dad clucked at me without looking up. As usual, his teeth were missing. He wore them to work, but he took them out as soon as he came home. He was probably resting his gums until it was time to eat. If I had caught a mess of fish, I would have bragged to him, but since I hadn't it was best not to say anything so I wouldn't get teased.

I walked into my room and closed the door.

Kirk Ohanian

My best friend at Garfield was Kirk. We were the same age and the stars of the basketball and softball teams. He was also my neighbor. It was a ritual for us to shoeshine together on Friday nights.

I picked up my shoeshine box and headed for his house by going down the stairs at the end of our dead-end street, and then up the hill on the worn path of the empty lot between Prospect Street and Jackson Street, where Kirk lived. Our houses were at eye level and nearly straight across from each other. Jackson Street was off Douglas Avenue, one of the better streets for shoeshining because of all the bars.

Our parents had accepted this latest craze of ours to make money for the things we wanted that our families couldn't afford to get for us. However, there was such a thing as *ahmoht*, and there was also such a thing as pride, and shoeshining made me question certain things I wasn't dying to look at.

There was something humiliating about shining shoes in a bar. I don't know if everyone felt that way, but I'm pretty sure all the Armenian kids did.

I didn't want to do anything that made me feel inferior. It was bad enough to be made to feel that way when I was in school, but there I didn't have a choice.

Kirk's dad worked at Belle City Foundry and had an even worse job than my dad's. My dad was a sweeper at J. I. Case. The foundries were hot, dirty, and dangerous. I don't know if it was because of the long hours he spent at work, or if it was because of Wisconsin's cold climate, but he was always complaining of drafts when he was at home. "Woman," he'd call to Kirk's mom, "again a draft has entered the room."

Mrs. Ohanian would come out of the kitchen and stand in the doorway, looking worried and confused. Without saying a word, she'd rush back into the kitchen and either bring him a cup of tea or a shawl for his shoulders. He'd sigh and then look up into her face, to see if his suffering had taken its proper effect on her.

I didn't like to spend any more time than was necessary at Kirk's house, so I usually stood by the kitchen door and waited for him to get ready.

Once we were safely out of his house, we began walking up Jackson Street toward Douglas Avenue. Kirk began talking about how well he thought we would do. "I feel like we ought to make a dollar each. Let's shoot for it, okay, Step?" I nodded my agreement and looked over at Kirk, who was feeling as anxious and nervous as I was about entering our first tavern of the night.

"The important thing is not to be too pushy," Kirk said.

"Where does that come from?" I said, because it didn't sound like it came from him.

"That's what Miss Baker said to me last year when she flunked me. 'Pushy people don't get ahead,' is how she put it. And then she said, 'Try to fit in.' Maybe it's good advice. We ought to give it a try if it helps us not to flunk."

"That's her opinion," I said. "Maybe if she stopped pushing us back, we'd stop pushing to get ahead. Anyhow, we're Armenians, and we couldn't behave like dried-up *odars* if we wanted to, which is what she is."

"No reason to be prejudiced about it," Kirk said.

"They started it," I said, "and unless they lay off, I'm going to finish it."

"Like heck you are. This ain't our country—it's theirs."

"It's as much ours as anybody's," I said. But I didn't believe it.

"Prove it," Kirk said.

"I don't have to," I said. "From now on when someone asks me my nationality, I'm going to say American."

"They'll only laugh at you."

"Well, it's technically correct," I said. "Nationality means the country of your birth, which is the country you are a citizen of. I looked it up."

"Well, forget it. You're an Armenian, and that's what you'll always be."

We turned left at the corner and headed up Douglas Avenue. It was dark out, and cold enough that we could see our breaths against the night air. I looked out at the flashing neon lights of the taverns up ahead.

Taverns were scary at night. They were dark, smoke-filled, and often noisy, with people talking all the time and the jukebox going strong. They had a funny smell as well, kind of stale and putrid, probably because the doors and windows were never opened. That's why we worked as a pair. We needed each other's moral support just to go inside.

We walked through the door of Charley's Bar and Grill and stopped to let our eyes adjust to the dark. I held my shoe box up in front of me with both hands. I had inscribed on the side of my box "A Shine for a Dime." A couple of the drinkers at the end of the bar looked up at us and then turned away. I approached a couple sitting by themselves at the bar, while I noticed out of the corner of my eye that Kirk was heading for one of the tables where a card game was going on.

"Would the lady like a shine?" I asked the man. The woman looked over at the man and smiled. He slowly and reluctantly turned and looked at me. He had high cheekbones and thin, mousy hair that fell unparted over his forehead. They didn't look married, so I felt I could count on a tip if the man said yes. "A shine for a dime," I offered.

"Go ahead, Doris," he allowed. "Give the little guy a break." He hadn't noticed that she had already shined her shoes for the evening. It was obvious that he had had enough to drink. She had a half-finished drink in front of her and a full one behind. His lone glass was empty.

"What school do you go to?" Doris said, extending her foot.

"Garfield," I muttered, reaching inside my box for brown Kiwi. She was wearing two-tone spectators. I would daub on the white liquid later, and if I was a little sloppy, it would be easier to remove my mistake with the tip of a clean rag over the new, greasy polish I was applying to the tips and heels.

"My son went to Garfield. He's at Washington Junior High now. Do you live on Liberty Street?" she asked. I could feel her staring down at my black, wavy hair. All of the homes on the first block of Liberty Street were occupied by Armenian families.

I said, "Uh-uh, Superior Street, ma'am."

I hated being talked to this way. I wished I had worn a hat. That way, if she looked down at my head , she wouldn't see me, but a piece of fabric. Maybe I'd inscribe something on it, like, "How would you know?" or "Not if the weather changes." Anything to get her attention off myself.

"You're going to like Washington Junior," she said.

"I'm going to like leaving Garfield," I said.

"I can tell you don't like it," she said. She had probably heard that the foreign kids were often flunked at Garfield Elementary.

She nudged her escort. "He's going to be happy to leave Garfield, Marvin. And probably the other one, too." She was looking over at Kirk, who had gotten a shine at one of the tables.

Marvin pretended he hadn't heard her. He was fingering his change on the bar when he realized that his glass was empty. He called to the bartender by rattling the remaining ice cubes in his glass. Doris reached in her purse and slipped me a quarter, as if it was a secret between us. It was a dime more than I expected, but I wasn't all that grateful under the circumstances.

We were standing on the sidewalk under the streetlight in front of Tony's tap, trying to enjoy the night air and looking up at a family of moths banging their stupid heads against the molded glass of the twin lights above our heads. We were considering which bar to hit next. "Did you feel *ahmoht* in there?" Kirk said.

"Why do you ask that?" I said. "There's nothing *ahmoht* about shining shoes."

"I know there's not," Kirk said, "but still, you know what I mean."

162

"If you don't brood on it, then it doesn't matter."

"I'm saving up for a football, right? You're saving up for a .22 rifle, right?"

"Right!"

"That's it, then. Forget it."

"It's forgotten," I said. "But what do you think would happen if an Armenian woman went into one of their taverns?"

"She'd be shipped back to the Old Country, I guess. Why, what do you think would happen?"

"I don't know," I said. "It wouldn't happen. I don't know why I thought of it."

"Why should we feel *ahmoht*, anyhow? It's stupid."

"Look how our dads have to work for a living."

"That's not *ahmoht*," Kirk said.

"Of course not. Who said it was?"

"I'm not working in no factory when I grow up."

"That makes two of us."

"I like to draw," I said.

"Like Rembrandt, I suppose," Kirk said, and laughed. "What say we shine shoes till we've got three dollars between us, and if it ain't too late we can go shoot a couple games of pool at Ace Grill."

"It's a deal," I said.

Ace Grill

I was watching Kirk line up the eight ball in the side pocket. It was a tough shot, but I was sure he would sink it, making it three games in a row. I had won the first game, at least. If this were the World Series of Pool, he'd have to win one more game before I won three straight in order to win the title. But it wasn't the World Series, it was a pickup game at Ace Grill, it was getting late, and three straight losses meant thirty cents out of my pocket. It was a good thing we weren't playing for anything on the side. The cost of the game was bad enough. But it was worth it, especially with school out for two whole days, and with a chance to make some extra money. I had just earned $1.65, and I could shine shoes again tomorrow night if I wanted. Saturday was movie day, and Sunday would be a pickup football game, or else I'd go over to the Tekeyans' and work on my scrapbook with Nicky.

The eight ball plopped into the side pocket, and I watched the cue ball bounce off the rails, hoping it would scratch. It didn't. I had to admit it: Kirk was the best. Not only at pool, but softball, football, basketball, and any other league game or pickup game we might think up. Not a lot better, but just better enough to be the undeclared champ. I was pretty darn good myself. In fact, we were one-two at all the team sports, and our team, Garfield, was the league champ in softball and basketball. And we figured to stay champs for the next two years.

We also had the oldest players in the league, which meant we were champs at flunking, too. Kirk and I were the stars, along with Harry Manoogian. Kirk had flunked three times to our two. Of course I didn't count flunking fifth twice, since it was the same grade, and the second time was summer school, so I only lost one year. We had already calculated how old we would be when we graduated from high school: Kirk twenty-one, me twenty, and Harry nineteen—but he would be twenty a month after graduation. At that rate it looked like we would be shaving before we even got out of grade school.

My mom was waiting up for me when I got home. I stopped in the doorway of the living room and looked in on her. She peered at me over her glasses, the lace doily she was making still in her hand. It was one of the things she was expert at. She made all her own presents to save money because my father made so little in the factory.

My mom didn't understand me, but she was the only person I

had to talk to, aside from Lily, and occasionally my uncle Mihran. I definitely couldn't talk to my dad. "Hello, *yavroos*," she said. "Is everything all right?"

"Of course, Mom. What did you expect?"

She didn't answer. I don't think she knew what she wanted for me, except that I be happy and safe. I looked up from the doily in her hand to the painting behind her of Mt. Ararat, the symbol of the Armenian nation. It seemed to surprise her when I asked, "Are the Turks like us?"

"Of course not. What a question. They murdered our tiny nation."

"But do they look like us? You know what I mean."

"They are Moslems. We are Christians."

"But are they dark like us, or are they maybe even darker?"

"About the same—some darker, some lighter. They are a mixed up race, not like us—pure! "My mother was darker than my father, and I took after her.

"So that wasn't it, then—they weren't prejudiced against us because we were different looking?"

"I told you—we were Christians."

"*That* was the prejudice?"

"Hatred! Discrimination!"

"We were aggressive, weren't we? Always trying to get ahead. Better than everyone else, always hustling."

"*Yavroos*, if you don't have your own country, it is harder, much harder. You can never understand. We were taxed, cheated, robbed. We had no rights in the courts. Nothing! We were violated. Someday you will understand. . . ."

"But we were the clever ones."

"We had to be."

And now it's happening here, I thought. In one way we'll always get by, in another way we'll never be equal. But I kept my mouth shut because my mother always defended America when we had these arguments. She didn't have to be an American, nor could she be an American, only a citizen of the United States. She was a foreigner. But I *was* an American, or rather an Armenian-American. Did being both make me neither, I wondered. Was that my nationality—neither? Is that why I was always uncomfortable with myself, with my parents, and also with the Americans?

"All of Me"

I slept in, as I always did on the weekend. By the time I got up, my father had already gone grocery shopping. My mother was in the kitchen, cutting away the fat on a shoulder of lamb. She stopped what she was doing and made *basturma* and eggs for breakfast.

"Toast or *choreg*?" she asked.

"*Choreg*," I said

"Tea or milk?"

"Milk—it's faster. I'm going to the Tekyans' just as soon as I pack my extra baseball cards."

When I pulled up on my bike, Nicky was sitting on the porch, reading the *Sporting News*. "Arpey's playing 'All of Me,'" again he said. I knew of course, what he meant. Arpey could play the same song fifty times in a row and never grow tired of it. We walked inside together at the very moment Arpey was leaving the living room to go upstairs. The record had stopped playing but was still winding to a stop on the turntable. Avak walked into the room with one of those look-out-here-I-come grins on his face. He removed the record and placed it under the cushion of the chair Arpey has been sitting in.

Nicky and I walked into the kitchen. We could hear his mom stirring ice cubes into a new pitcher of lemonade—her specialty.

When we walked back into the living room with our glasses, Arpey was coming down the stairs. Lily and Eva were seated on the sofa, discussing the latest feature attraction at the Rialto Theater, and

Avak had taken a chair in the corner of the room. He said very casually, "Arpey, don't sit down in that chair again." Arpey looked over at Avak and placed her hand on the arm of the club chair she had been sitting in. She smiled defensively.

"That's right," Eva said. "Don't sit in that chair."

"Why not?" Arpey said, still smiling.

"I wouldn't sit there if I were you," Nicky said.

"Not a good idea, Arpey," Avak said. "Don't do it."

Lily remained silent, calculating the scene and trying not to get involved.

Arpey took a step forward in front of the chair, pretending she was about to sit down.

"Uh-uh," Avak, Eva, and Nicky said in succession. "Better not, Arpey."

"Don't do it," I said, speaking for the first time, and like the others not meaning a word of what I said.

"Why shouldn't I?" Arpey said. Her smile by now was turning into a grimace.

"Can't tell you," Avak said, "but I know you don't want to sit in that chair."

"I *do* want to," Arpey said.

"You *don't* want to," Nicky said.

"You don't know what I want," Arpey said.

"Oh, yes I do," Avak said, "all too well."

Arpey sat down, but so slowly and cautiously that for an instant nothing happened. But then, all at once, we heard the faint but unmistakable sound that only a splitting, cracking record can make.

Arpey sprang up from her chair. She didn't utter a word at first, but she had a terrible, ghastly look on her face. Then she slowly lifted the cushion and stared down at the shattered record.

"We told you not to sit down," Avak said—before being drowned out by her screams.

"We didn't do it, Arpey," Eva said. "*You* did it."

"Monsters, devils, beasts," Arpey screamed. "I hate all of you." She continued screaming as she ran up the stairs.

"She'll get another one," Eva said.

"But not immediately," Avak said.

"That was great," Nicky said. "No question, she had it coming."

Lily was the only one who looked unhappy. She got up and walked to the stairs. Unlike her brothers and sisters, Lily had her own room. It wasn't long before she began playing her cello. She was saving up to go to Juilliard so she could become a classical musician. At least that's what everyone said. Lily never talked about it herself. She was very private, and also a loner, like me, which was probably why I liked her and also looked up to her.

I was visualizing Lily's bow moving across the strings of her cello. The music was sad but not in the least mournful. It kept growing in intensity without losing any of its softness. I could feel Lily's presence in the room over our heads, but when I looked up I realized that I was the only one listening to the music.

Tyrone Power

Nicky had gone back to the porch with the Sporting News under his arm. Avak was in the kitchen, and Eva was ironing again in the living room. I walked outside and sat next to Nicky, who was staring off into space. "Want to see a movie?" he said, turning to look at me.

"Sure," I said. "What's playing?"

"The *Mark of Zorro* with Tyrone Power, at the Venetian."

"Your mother says he's Armenian."

"Wishful thinking. He's got black hair and he's dark complected, so she put two and two together and made it up."

"He's handsome," I said.

"That's why she's hoping he's Armenian. Akim Tamaroff is the only Armenian in Hollywood. He's short, fat, and has a big nose."

"He's not exactly ugly," I said.

"Not exactly, but he's no Tyrone Power."

"But the director's Armenian," I said. "Rouben Mamoulian. He's one of the best."

"I don't like his movies."

"I don't either. Should we go?"

"Yeah. Afterward we can trade baseball cards. If you want, you can stay over. Take your bike around to the back, why don't ya?" Nicky didn't ride anymore. He was two years older than me and in the ninth grade from never having flunked. The difference in our age and all didn't matter, though, because our mothers were best friends and so there was never a time when we didn't know each other.

We walked up La Salle Street to State. We might have taken the shortcut through the coal yards on Huron Street, but we didn't. We continued straight on and crossed the State Street bridge, which was my favorite bridge because the river is at its widest at this point and makes one last sweeping turn before it empties into Lake Michigan.

We leaned on the green railing and watched the boats and the sea gulls while staring down at the muddy water that was full of carp and bullheads.

Nicky didn't feel the way I did about bridges and waterways. He preferred Lake Michigan, where you could lie on the beach and go swimming. But what I liked about water was that it helped me to dream. I could follow Root River with my imagination and let it take me to all the places of the world I had never been, but would someday go to. In my mind one river led to another, and even if one emptied into a lake now and then, it didn't stop there but was connected on the opposite shore with another river, and from there the journey continued. Rivers were passageways to the unknown. Lakes were more like cities, where one stopped and stayed. But I didn't want to stay anywhere. I wanted to go, to be on my way

169

without any particular destination in mind. Someday I would stay, when I found my true home and place in the world, but I couldn't imagine when that would be, or where it would be, so I was going to be content to travel, upriver and down, until I knew who I was and what I wanted to be.

When we got to the Venetian, it was too early to go in. The *Mark of Zorro* had a half hour to go, so they weren't seating anyone.

"Should we go over to the Park Arcade?" Nicky said. "Or go across the street to Monument Square?" Nicky liked pinball games, but he didn't like pool, and it was vice versa with me.

"Let's go sit on that bench by the pool," I said. "That way we won't have to keep track of the time. We'll see the people leaving the theater when it's over." I liked sitting on the park benches with a buddy because Monument Square was the heart of downtown, and this was the city's busiest corner. Monument Square consisted of two pools and a monument. Its rectangular shape took up nearly a square block of space. I didn't know about Nicky, but I felt like a big shot sitting there and surveying the city, which I could imagine was some famous place—and not the place it actually was—and that I was famous, too, or at least interesting and important, though I couldn't think how I could be interesting and important, so all I could do was pretend to be somebody else.

"What do you want to be when you grow up?" I asked Nicky.

"A major leaguer."

"Me too," I said. "Frankie Crosetti."

"Good field, no hit."

"He can't hit the curve ball, and neither can I. But I'm working on it. Anyhow, you only get to bat like four times a game, when you play the infield you might see the ball that many times or more in one inning. Shortstop, that's my position for life. How about you?"

"Ernie Lombardi," Nicky said. "The catcher sees the ball on every pitch. He handles the pitcher and directs the team. The only position more important is the pitcher, but I want to play every day."

Ernie Lombardi was the slowest runner in either league. He had never stolen a base and couldn't bunt. He was short and stocky, like Nicky, but he could hit the long ball—sometimes.

The movie theater was starting to empty out. From where we were sitting, we could see people streaming out the side door exit.

"No hurry," Nicky said. "It'll be a while before the comings start."

It wasn't long before the bakery next door to the Venetian was packed with people. Most of them would be buying kringle to have with their Sunday breakfasts.

For some reason I felt great inside. We were about to see a movie that was directed by an Armenian, and even if we didn't like it, there were bound to be things about it we did like. And besides, it was Saturday and we had almost a full day and a half before school would begin again.

Private Bakaian

My father shopped on Saturdays and cooked on Sundays. He had learned to cook in the Army, and after his discharge he had become a short-order cook at the Nelson Hotel. That was before he met my mother. Because after they were married she made him leave Nelson's and go into the factory, where he could work regular hours and have the weekends off—unlike Nelson's, where he had worked the night shift and only had one day off a week, if he was lucky.

But cooking was what he was meant to do. And what he would never do again—except on Sundays. I had come to the conclusion a long time before that my dad wasn't a fighter. If he were, he would have gotten himself a restaurant or even a dinky diner somewhere, like the White Tower, where he would have been his own boss and done work that was his own and that he was meant to do. I never discussed this with him. Instead, I argued about it with my mom because I felt like she was standing in his way. But she always said the same thing: He can't because he doesn't read English. . . . It's not his country. . . . He's lucky to be working and supporting a family. . . . It's what everyone else is doing. . . .We are lucky to have a roof over our heads and food on the table.

I didn't believe her, although there were some days when I would weaken and half believe her. But even then I found it unacceptable. Because if it was true for him, then maybe it would be true for me also. Rebelling in school wasn't getting me anywhere. Maybe rebelling as an adult would produce the same result. How could I know? How could I be sure of anything?

The dining room table was set for four, but Uncle Mihran hadn't yet arrived. My mother was in the living room, the farthest room from the kitchen, embroidering one of her hankies. She was sitting at the end of the couch on the one seat where she could see into the kitchen. She was making a mistake, because if my father wanted to he could see her as well. She was his enemy on Sundays, and he was her nuisance.

It was their house, but except for Sundays she had it all to herself. She hardly made a sound when she cooked, but when he cooked the kitchen became a showplace for disorder, with everything being used at once, and effectively, although you'd never know it by appearances. Uncle Mihran said my dad was an artist—and if the results of his cooking were the proof, then there was no doubt that Uncle MIhran was right. My mother was pleased with the food but not by his other artistic results.

His one mistake was asking my mother where things were kept. He never could find anything when he needed it, and when he needed something he needed it *now*. If she could have produced what he wanted without a sound, it might have been okay, but she couldn't do that. She had only to utter a single comment—as she always did—and he would commence to roar like a wounded lion, pick up a knife, and chase her around the kitchen table and out of

172

the room. He of course didn't hear a word she said.

But I did! And I tried to see it from both her side and his. I wasn't in agreement with either of them. I would scream for peace because peace was all *I* wanted. I simply couldn't understand that he didn't mean anything by chasing her with a knife. I thought he meant it. I thought he meant to kill her. And that it was only a matter of time before he would.

Whenever I entered the house on Sunday afternoons—and I made it a point to stay away for as long as I could—I'd check the walls to see if they had been sprayed with blood. By now I knew better, but that didn't help how I felt about their fights, and my worries over my mother's safety.

I had learned from an incident that had happened early in the summer that my father did not intend to harm my mother, only to threaten her. It was natural, I learned that he would do it with a knife. It had to do with his background. I had come to this conclusion during the *Madagh*, our annual church picnic, when I saw my father performing a solo dance with a knife clenched tightly between his teeth. I was scared at first, if not terrified, but somehow with the music playing, the people clapping and chanting, it seemed in some odd way to be natural—that is, natural for an Armenian. And some part of me could see that it was not really crazy at all.

I tried to think what it all meant, and I finally came to the conclusion that knives were the common weapons used by the Armenians in the Old Country, since they were not allowed to bear arms in Turkey. For that reason probably everyone carried a knife. I remembered that in photos I had seen they carried their knives in the cummerbunds, so they would be handy in an emergency. Isn't that what the cowboys did in the movies—reach for their guns whenever anything was in doubt? And if they didn't reach for them, they fingered them slyly or looked down at them tucked neatly in their holsters, ready for action.

I wasn't sure if my mom and dad had already had their fight

when I walked into the house, but at least there wasn't any blood on the kitchen walls. I knew better than to check, but I couldn't help myself. I peered into the kitchen and nonchalantly looked things over. My father, at that moment, wasn't even cooking. He was staring out the kitchen window while puffing on a cigarette. When he saw me, he walked into the dining room and sat down." Everything rest now," he said in English. "Maybe I'm resting it now, too."

I was glad to see he was in a good mood. "Chicken?" I said, because that's what he usually cooked on Sundays. He nodded, pleased with himself and his afternoon of work. "Tell me about the first time you cooked chicken," I said. It was an old story, but I never tired of hearing it.

"Not first time, first time officers' mess." This was an American story, and he was using English to tell it.

"I was cooking in the kitchen full-time," he began, creating the setting in our language. "We were cooking chicken. For the troops we'd cut the chickens up into parts, but for the officers we had to serve the chicken whole. That wasn't my job. That was the job of the head cook, who made it special, cooking the officers' chickens himself, adding this and that, and then serving them on a special platter, carving them at the table, and so. But the head cook was hung over. He couldn't cook. He was still in the sack. So they told me, 'Bedros, you cook the officers' chicken today' "

"So you served the chicken that day?" I said.

"That's right. I cook chicken, I serve chicken, and so on."

"What happened next?" I asked, trying to keep a straight face.

"Time passes, yes. We're cleaning up. The Lieutenant walks into kitchen and says it to me, 'Bedros, the Captain wants to see you' ."

"What's I do wrong? I thinks me. If Captain mad, bring trouble, yes. I quick remove apron, roll down sleeves, and so on. I follow Lieutenant into officers' mess. I come up to Captain's table." At this point my father stopped speaking and got to his feet, placing his cig-

174

arette in the ashtray.

He clicked his heels and stood at rigid attention.

Then he saluted and spoke. "Private Bakaian reporting, sir."

"Private Bakaian," the Captain answers. But I cannot be sure from my father's voice what the Captain is feeling. Is he puzzled, is he amused, is he curious? Who is this Private Bakaian? Maybe there is a question in his voice.

"Yes, sir," my father answers, nervous now but beginning to swell with pride because he knows what is coming next.

"Very good chicken I eat today, Private Bakaian. I ask, who cook this chicken? They tell me Private Bakaian, he cook it. Is that so?"

"Yes, sir," my father says once again, his eyes staring straight ahead, the color rising in his face.

"I want start you tomorrow cook officers' mess. Be my cook from now on."

"Yes, sir!" my father says for the last time, and once again he salutes and clicks his heels. But this time he is unable to turn around as he had done then, so very long ago. His chair is directly behind him, so he sits down. He smiles to himself, picks up his cigarette from the ashtray, and flicks the ash, his face flushed with happiness.

It was a thrilling story, and I never tired of hearing it. It was my father's one moment of triumph in a life of frustration. At least that's how I saw it. But it was more than that for me. It was much, much more for me than that. What it told me was that if they know you are good, you will be rewarded. Ability is what counts. If you're good at something, if you're the best, then that's it, you can do what you want. No one will stop you.

But I wasn't sure I believed it. Yet I wanted to believe it. I wanted so badly to believe that it was true that I *did* believe it— almost!

The Armenian Fence

Another horrible year of school had come to an end. But this time I made it. I passed the fifth grade at last, which meant that I had only one year left at Garfield.

It was summer again, my favorite season of the year. The garden had been dug, and my dad was getting ready to put his seeds in the ground. But first he decided it was time we painted our fence. "What color you think it we paint fence?" he asked me one morning over breakfast. I was naturally suspicious because he had just spoken in English.

"Do you want my help?" I asked without committing myself.

"Of course," my mother said. "Father and son, you can do it together."

"Blue," I said.

"Naturally," my mother said, "your favorite color."

My father looked from my mother to me without speaking. "Is that the right color for a fence?" he said. "Let us consider for a moment. Blue! The sky is blue. Every day we see the sky. Every day we look at something blue. Should we have a fence also colored blue? What color blue did you have in mind?'

"Light blue," I said.

"That's his favorite color," my mother said without turning from the stove.

My father dunked his *choreg* in his coffee and thought to himself. "Maybe," he said at last, "you shouldn't waste your favorite color on a fence."

"He doesn't think blue is appropriate," my mother said to me, as if the discussion only involved the two of us.

"What color did you have in mind?" I asked my dad. He pronounced an Armenian word that wasn't in my vocabulary. "I haven't the English word," I said.

"It is between yellow and brown," my mother said.

176

"You mean ocher," I said. "That's a pretty strange color for a fence—or for anything else. In this country, at least."

My father dunked his *choreg* in his coffee and didn't speak. I dunked mine in my tea. We were staring at each other across the table. He finished his *choreg* and downed the rest of his coffee. I didn't say anything. After a couple of minutes he pushed his chair away from the table and stood up. He was still in his BVD's, and barefoot, as usual.

After he had walked into the bedroom to get dressed, my mother turned from the stove and spoke to me in a whisper. "It reminds him of the Old Country. Try not to make a fight."

"I'm not looking to make a fight, but ocher's an ugly color. I mean, nobody has ever painted a fence ocher. It's unheard of. Can't we find something else to remind him of the Old Country?"

"Don't be impossible. He wants your help. And he wants an Armenian color for the fence. The garden reminds him of Armenia, the dirt reminds him of his village, the vegetables he grows remind him of his home in Kharpet. That's why he's so angry. He's tormented by remembering, and he feels tormented when he forgets. Let him have his way."

At the hardware store I asked the clerk to show us the paint chart. I went down the chart till I found ocher. I showed the color swatch to my dad. "What do you think?"

"It needs a little brown, and a touch of red."

"I don' think they mix that way," I said.

"Why not?"

"It's not a standard color. They can't guarantee the result."

"I'll guarantee it. Two drops of brown, one drop of red. Two gallons. I don't need to see it—just have him mix it."

I told the clerk what my dad had said. He looked us up and down, smiled weakly, and disappeared into the back room.

"No problem," I said to my dad.

"You will see," my father said. "We have picked the right color for a fence."

The Armenian School

I could no longer get out of attending Armenian School classes. They were held Wednesday evenings in the cellar of the Armenian church on State Street.

My mother hadn't pressured me to attend before now because she knew I didn't want to go. But it must have been hard for her to make excuses for me, since she was one of the two regular teachers.

The church cellar, whose entrance was on Wilson Street, consisted of a hallway, with a kitchen and bathroom on either side, opening out into an auditorium-sized room with a raised platform for plays, speeches, recitations, and the like. Inside this space, along the wall facing Wilson Street, were two rooms that were used for a variety of purposes: cloak and storage rooms, including multiple purpose rooms. On Wednesday evenings two of these were quickly converted into classrooms for beginning and advanced pupils.

What was being taught was the language itself; that is, reading, writing, and pronunciation. For although everyone spoke Armenian at home, nearly everyone was illiterate, not only the children, but their parents as well.

My mother had presented me with the book I would be using before she went off to class ahead of me. I sat down on my bed and looked it over. There were drawings ornamenting each of the letters, with additional drawings throughout the book. It wasn't so different from the books I remembered in the first grade, except that the people being drawn were Armenians, not Americans, and the scenes that were depicted were of another country. I wondered if the country was Armenia, since I had never before seen pictures of my parents' homeland, except for a few snapshots.

It was obvious that our grammar book had not been produced in America. Everything about it, from the binding to the paper to the drawings and printing, seemed Old Country, which was only another word in my vocabulary for "backward."

At the same time it had a feeling of familiarity, but of what I wasn't sure. After all, I had spoken only Armenian until my mother sent me to nursery school at age four, which meant that Armenian was my mother tongue.

When I got to the church, the class of older students had just been let out. They were milling about, waiting for the next class to begin.

"Look who's here," Hatch Kevorkian said when I walked into the room, "*Deegen* Zabel's boy. So you finally broke down."

I shrugged my shoulders and looked around the room. If I was going to be razzed, then no matter what I said it would only be used against me.

"Don't pay him any attention," Rose Parsegian, one of the older girls, said to me.

"I'm not," I said. "It's a free country. He can say whatever he likes."

"You're not too good for us, are you?" Peter Baleozian said.

"Maybe I'm not good enough for you," I said. "Isn't that what you really mean?"

"I don't know," Pete said. "I only know you never come around for church services, you don't belong to any of the clubs, you never act in the plays. . . ."

"What is he, on trial?" Rose said. "He hasn't been here two minutes, and already you're on his back."

"That's okay," I said. "I can take it. Pete's entitled to his opinion, small as it is. What I do with my free time is my business. If some people want to go from home to church and back again, they've got that right. And I've got the right not to."

Rose didn't agree with me, so she shut up. Probably no one agreed with me.

My mother clapped her hands to indicate that it was time for classes to resume. I didn't like the expression on her face. I could tell that she had been listening to our conversation. She took the older class, and Mrs. Avakian took our class of beginners.

I felt like I was in the first grade again. Except this time the lessons were easy. We opened our books to the first page. "*Aye, pen, keem*," Mrs. Avakian said, and paused before repeating with her thick accent, "A, B, C." She then recited the thirty-six letters of our alphabet.

Mrs. Avakian went from the recitation of the alphabet to different drills to help us memorize the letters. Before long we were writing out the letters and practicing our penmanship, which was one of the few things I had enjoyed in regular school. I felt comfortable with the other kids and not the least bit threatened. But I also felt stifled, being in such a small room. I didn't like the smell of the cellar any more than I liked the smell of the church floor above. It made me feel sad.

I got home before my mother did. I was sitting in the living room reading when she walked in the door. I watched her remove her hat and hang up her coat. She went into the kitchen to speak to my dad before walking back through the dining room and then into the living room, where she took a seat across from me. She was waiting for me to tell her about the class, but she could see that I didn't want to discuss it. "You're not like the others," she said.

"I know."

"Why aren't you like the others?"

"I wish I knew, but I don't."

"What is it that's bothering you?"

"You wouldn't understand."

"If I don't know what's bothering you, I can't possibly understand, can I?"

"I don't want to be a sad Armenian. I don't like being looked down on. I feel backward and unwanted, and it's worse when I'm with the Armenians."

"They embarrass you."

"Yes."

"You know how your face looks when you're in church?"

"No," I said. "I have no idea."

"Frightened. You don't look out of place, but you do look frightened. What is that about?"

I had to think. I was also trying to decide what to tell her and what not to tell her. I didn't like the look of worried concern on her face. It made me feel bad. My mother always listened to me and encouraged me, and I knew she believed in me, even if I did drive her crazy most of the time. I owed her an explanation. "I guess my biggest fear is that I'm going to starve to death. That I'm going to be abandoned, lying in the streets, with nowhere to turn, and that I'm slowly going to starve."

"*Yavroos*, we came to this country so we *wouldn't* starve. That will never happen here."

"I don't think about it all the time. It just pops into my head sometimes."

"Is that your big fear?"

"No. I don't have any big fears, unless it's that I'm going to be stuck here when it's time for me to leave, and when that happens I'll end up working in a factory and never get to know the world and all the people living in it."

"I didn't know you felt that way."

"I'm not sure I know what I mean. I'm not even sure I know what I want. I just know what I *don't* want."

"You're saying that you don't belong here."

"I won't always be here is what I mean. I don't know if there is any place where I belong, but I believe there will be such a place, depending on what I do with my life. I just know whatever it is I need to happen, it can never happen here."

"Thirteen years old, and already such big thoughts."

"What kind of thoughts did you have at thirteen?"

"Much different. I was very old at thirteen. I missed my childhood. I never completed my childhood. With one part of me I wanted to go back. With another part I did what had to be done. I was *jarbeek*. I always took the next step."

"You were a survivor."

My mother looked at me for a long minute. "I am a part of two worlds, one lost and shattered, the other a compromise. Now you tell me it is the same with you."

"It's not your fault," I said. "It's just the way it is."

"I don't want you to be lonely."

"That's not one of my fears," I said. "I've always been lonely."

BOOK TWO

Baseball Cards

Of the two hundred Armenian families in Racine the most interesting by far—in my opinion—are the Tekeyans. Nicky's father was one of the few Armenian men who didn't work in a factory. He owned a restaurant-bar on Douglas Avenue that he ran with his brother. Compared to us, they were rich, which was why Arpey could buy as many records and movie magazines as she liked and why Nicky could play the pinball games. But it wasn't money that made them interesting—it was something else. They had style and intelligence. And also they were eccentric. On top of that they were miserable—but each in his own way, so that when they were all together they really made a scene. It was better than going to a movie or a play. A feeling of excitement came over me whenever I was in their home, because without even trying they were teaching me about books, movies, jazz, art, and all kinds of other things that most people I knew didn't ever think about.

Although they were inspiring to me, they weren't inspiring to themselves. Nicky's father, Krikor, was always hollering at Nicky's mom because she never stayed home, and she was mad at him for throwing his money around. The children were angry with their mom because she seldom cooked or cleaned house, and they were mad at their father for the same reason their mother was—and also because he was never home, either.

But why Nicky and his brother and sisters were unhappy with themselves was hard to figure out. Avak was angry because of what the Armenians had been through, which they were always reminding him of, which he said was interfering with his life. And so he didn't know where he was going or what to do with himself. Eva felt unloved, and Arpey was sick all the time (The Armenians said her

183

mother tried to abort her and the medicines she took while she was pregnant had permanently damaged her). Lily didn't have the privacy she needed, and although she was supposed to be going off to Juilliard, so far she hadn't left home. Avak was in his last year of high school, and the girls had all graduated. Nicky wasn't miserable—he was just sad, but he was trying to fight his way out of it.

The funny thing, I guess, was that they never affected me the way they affected themselves. Like I said, they were the most exciting Armenian family in town.

Sunday was the saddest day of the week. The city was dead. Everyone was locked up in their homes. The church bells rang mournfully, the people dressed unnaturally, and everything seemed to be out of kilter. Also, except in summer, it was the last day of freedom before school began again for another week. The only good thing about Sunday was that it was the best day to visit Nicky and his family because all of them were likely to be home.

My mom and dad always went to church on Sundays. I liked being alone in the mornings because that was the best time to draw and write in my diary. But I wanted to leave the house before they got back and before my father began cooking the Sunday dinner.

I carried my bike onto Nicky's porch and leaned it against the rails. There was a discussion going on in the living room, and on the record player in the dining room there was an Armenian record playing. It was Shah-Mouradian, Nicky's father's favorite, singing one of the Old Country songs that's so sad it makes you wish you were dead. I followed Nicky into his bedroom, where the ball game was on—Yanks versus the White Sox—which is how I knew for sure he'd be home. "It's a lucky thing we saved our baseball cards," Nicky said, closing the door.

"Yeah," I said, and waited for him to tell me why.

"Now we can try to perfect our card collections. Have a look at the back of this comic. It lists all the ones produced so far. A perfect collection consists of two hundred twenty-five."

"How many do you have?"

"Over one hundred fifty."

"That's way more than me. I'll never make it."

"Want to trade your cards for something else, like one of my board games? Or some movie magazines?"

"Those are all Arpey's."

"She'll never know. I'll help you steal them."

"Nah," I said. "I think I'll hang on to the cards I've got. I like going over them."

"Think DiMaggio will break the consecutive game hitting record?" Nicky said.

"He only needs three more games."

"Two. He got a hit in the first inning. Let's bet something on how far he'll go. What's your guess?"

"No fair," I said. "The guy that goes first doesn't stand a chance. If I say forty, you'll say forty-one, so then anything higher than forty you automatically win."

"But if it's under forty, you win."

"Yeah, but it's nearly that now."

"Then guess fifty."

"O, yeah, I know you. You'll guess forty-nine."

"He could top fifty," Nicky said.

"Fat chance," I said. "Even DiMaggio couldn't get a hit in fifty straight games."

"Let's go have some lemonade and a Spam sandwich," Nicky said. "Lily just brought home some fresh *peda*."

All the time we had been talking, I was watching Avak through the cracked door. The discussion in the living room had turned into a shouting match. Avak was biting down hard on his index finger of his fisted hand, which was his way of restraining himself from committing violence. I was watching in amazement, and suddenly I saw that he had two strangers living inside himself that were of equal strength—one invisible (the good guy) who was causing him to revolt, and the other (the bad guy) who was doing the revolting and making trouble, not with others but within himself. His face had slowly turned red, and now his neck was bulging out. He was stomping across the room while alternately cursing and biting his finger, with violent restraint. "Avak's raging again in the other room," I said to Nicky.

"Don't pay any attention. Just follow me into the kitchen."

"He never hollers at me," I said.

"That's not the point. Just don't look at him, so he doesn't think he has an audience."

"Got ya," I said. "I'll sneak in behind you."

Nicky walked toward the kitchen through the living room, but when he passed Avak, who was ranting away, he gave him a sidearm punch with the back of the clenched fist of his right hand. Avak wheeled around and landed a punch on Nicky's forearm and gave out a roar of pleasure. Nicky crouched into his boxer's stance—he had been secretly working out in the YMCA gym, hoping to compete in the Golden Gloves—and threw two quick punches into Avak's midriff. Avak parried with two well-aimed body shots of his own, cursing with pleasure, while Nicky smiled wolfishly to himself. Avak burst out laughing. "C'mon, fatso," he bellowed, "put 'em up." He was still grinding away on his index finger. He threw a series of staccato punches with his left, while shouting. "Who do you think you are to challenge your big brother? Haven't you any respect? I'll destroy you. I'll turn you into mincemeat for *kufta*, you sheepherder, you Armenian cucumber."

Nicky faked a shot to the stomach, faked a shot to the head, and landed a one-two punch, left, right, to Avak's forearm—and declared himself the winner by strutting away, as if his brother had just been liquidated. Avak ran beside him, wheeled around, and gave him a swift kick in the rear with the back of his foot that sent Nicky stumbling into the kitchen. I followed quickly behind and got between them, sticking two fingers in my mouth, and whistling an end to the fight.

Mr. Huber

It was the first day of school. Sixth grade. One more year, and I'd be on my way to Washington Junior—and whatever lay beyond.

But I had gotten off on the wrong foot again. We weren't in the room fifteen minutes when I got sent out to the hall. Our teacher, Miss Simpson, wanted to seat us alphabetically, which would put me in the front seat, one row over from the window.

"I want to sit by the window," I said, "and I don't want to sit in the front seat." I hadn't bothered to raise my hand to ask permission to speak.

"Well!" she exclaimed. "I see you haven't learned anything about conduct after five grades in our school, but I will see to it that you learn how to behave in *my* class, or else. Just go sit in the hall, young man, until I decide to have you in my room."

I was so mad I could have spit. I didn't see why I should be punished for speaking my mind. Even if everyone else kept their mouths shut tight, it didn't make keeping my mouth shut the right thing to do. I was old enough to have certain rights myself.

The janitor walked by and shook his head at me, as if I were some kind of hopeless case. I followed him with my eyes and scowled. He didn't scare me.

All kinds of thoughts were going through my head, none of them worth repeating out loud. All at once I remembered that we were supposed to get a new principal. When I first heard the rumor, I had hoped it was true, because whoever came along it would have to be an improvement over the principal we had—old man Snyder, who had never learned any of our names or taken the least interest in our activities, especially our school-yard activities, like sports.

At that moment I looked up to see a tall man in a pin-striped suit, with bow tie, come marching down the hall. He glanced at me as he hurried by. I still had the scowl on my face that I had put on for the janitor.

To my surprise he turned around—after he had walked out of my sight—and came back and stood facing me.

I didn't bother to change my expression. He said, "How would you like to catch some fungoes?"

I was almost too startled to speak. But I didn't hesitate for long, even though I only half believed he was telling the truth. When we got to his office, I was surprised to see a bat and ball in the corner by his desk.

Without saying a word to his secretary, he grabbed up his equipment—which included a mitt for me—and we started down the steps to the school yard.

"Tell me your name," he said, as we walked out the door. "Mine's Max Huber."

"Sure, Mr. Huber," I said, "but it's kind of complicated. I'm Stepan to my parents, and Steven to my teachers and some of the others, but my friends call me Step."

"Okay, Step," Mr. Huber said. "What would you like, grounders or fly balls?"

"Grounders," I said. "I'm an infielder."

Mr. Huber was holding the bat over his shoulder with his left hand while tossing the ball up and catching it with his right. "You're not in position," he said.

"Oh!" I answered, and realized that he was right. I quickly crouched and slammed my fist into the glove, improving the pocket. My heart was thumping so loudly it frightened me.

He hit a weak grounder in front of me. I came charging in and took it bare-handed and looped it back to him.

"Good play," he called out. "I think you had him at first."

"Home plate, too," I said, "if there had been a runner on third trying to score." I slammed my glove again, making it pop.

He hit the next several grounders really hard, and I made clean pickups each time. I was so charged up I didn't think I'd ever make an error on any ball I could put a glove on.

The next grounders he hit were to my left. Some were easy pickups, and others I had to work hard to reach. I still hadn't let one get by me.

"You're doing good," Mr. Huber said, but this time he hit one to my right. I knocked it down backhanded and picked it up at once. "I would have had him at first," I shouted.

He hit another to my right, but this time I flubbed it. "You don't go to your right as well as to your left," Mr. Huber shouted.

"No one does."

"That's no reason for you not to," he shouted back, and hit a fiery grounder that nearly went through my legs. "Do you know why?"

"It's hard to turn the glove in reverse and still have control over the pocket," I said.

"That's half of it, "Mr. Huber said. "You're in such a hurry to go to your right that you take your eye off the ball. That's not true when you go to your left, if you've noticed."

"I think you're right," I said. "Thanks."

"We'll work on it sometime," Mr. Huber said. "My secretary's been at the window for ten minutes now, trying to get my attention. We'd better go back inside."

I kept pounding the glove as we walked to the front door and up the stairs, and I nearly forgot to give it back when we got to his office. "Here," I said, "and thanks a lot for the game."

Mr. Huber turned and smiled at me. "Keep your eye on the ball," he said, and disappeared inside his office.

I took my seat outside the door of my classroom. I was glad to be alone, and I no longer felt embarrassed. All kinds of thoughts were flying around in my head. I was sure I had learned something big, but I couldn't say that I knew what it was. Mr. Huber had made me feel important, and that was enough in itself, because I realized that I had never felt that way in all the years I had been at Garfield.

Scout's Woods

October has always been my favorite month. The autumn leaves turn color, and when they do, everything seems to grow quiet and there is a feeling that the elements of nature are beginning to return to where they belong.

The place I liked to go to when I wanted to be alone was Scout's Woods, which began at the edge of town where State Street turned into Highway 38. To get there, you had to cross two open fields that were divided by a row of abandoned apple trees. From there the land sloped abruptly into a wooded area. On the side of the hill that ran down to the river was a natural spring, where I always stopped to have a drink. At the bottom of the slope there was a marshy area caused by the continual flow of water from the spring. I sometimes walked across the log that had fallen over the marsh, or else took the long walk around it. It was a popular spot for game animals and birds, with woodcocks favoring the slope below the spring, ducks preferring the marsh, and rabbits and pheasants the field just beyond that bordered the river. I'd never walked from the spring to the river without flushing game, and it was always a shock and a thrill when it happened.

But my destination, if I had one, was the swinging bridge that skirted the wild fields at the edge of the golf course. At that time of year there were never more than one or two pairs of golfers on the course, and their dress and movements seemed to blend with the flow of the land and nature's changing colors. And they were friendly in a way that they never were in the summer, when they made me feel that I was intruding on their sacred property.

I liked to wear a parka when I went tramping, not only for the warmth but also because it seemed the right garment to wear in the outdoors. I also liked to wear it because it had two big pockets, one for the sandwich that I always made myself and wrapped in wax paper, and the other for my notebook—because I always wrote and sketched when I went by myself to Scout's Woods. When I reached the middle of the bridge, I sat down with my legs dangling over the side, facing upstream, away from the golf course. I looked down at the water and let its stillness enter me, feeling inspired by the sense of oneness in things, because it seemed at the moment that I was a part of everything that was. I opened my notebook and started to write.

> Why does the river turn black at this season of the year and seem to slow and grow quiet and wait? Is it returning to its source or settling into itself—as the leaves settle to the ground around the tree that bore them, where they will rest and wait until they rise and turn again into leaves, as you must settle, gentle river, into this season of dying, until you flow again at the passing of winter, at the coming of a new spring. . . .

I didn't hear the golfers approaching until their footsteps rattled the bridge. One of them said, "You've got a good day for it, son."

I closed my notebook. "Sure," I said. "I guess you do, too."

"Every warm day is a gift from now on," the other golfer said.

"You've got the course to yourselves," I said.

"So have you," the first one said.

"I know," I said. "That's the way I like it."

They both laughed good-naturedly. And then they were gone. I stuck my notebook in my pocket and crossed the bridge onto the golf course. I thought I'd go sit on a bunker and eat my sandwich and see what the gophers were up to. Maybe I'd make a sketch of one of them, or else just draw the trees.

The Bridge and Park

It was November, the saddest time of the year, being neither autumn nor winter. I decided to take a walk to the park that was just three blocks from our house. It overlooked Main Street, with a view of Lake Michigan in the distance. It was a small triangular park perched on a knoll, and its lone bench was almost always vacant during the late afternoons on Fridays, because everyone was cashing their checks and shopping or getting spruced up for the evening. It meant I could be alone with my thoughts, undisturbed, and with a chance to look out on the city without being noticed by anyone.

When I got to the park, two dogs were chasing each other through the bushes that bordered the lower corner, near the fountain. I moved the lone bench to give myself the view I wanted and sat down.

The State Street bridge in the distance had just opened, and the boat it had let through seemed to grow in size as it headed in my direction. It must have been carrying food because it was being shadowed by sea gulls. I followed the river with my eyes, from the State Street bridge to the Main Street bridge, which lay directly beneath my view.

Beyond the river, the cars moved swiftly in opposite directions, with more of them heading toward the downtown than away from it. I followed their movement until my sight was blocked by the building at the corner of Main and State, where I was able to make out the roof of the Main Street Theatre, and also the facade of the bowling alley that had once been the Rex Theatre during the days of silent movies.

I began to wonder, as I had so often, why it seemed that everything was more possible at such moments. I looked down at the river and dreamed its meaning. It seemed so different from ours. Whenever I dreamed the river I dreamed myself, not as I was, with all my problems, but as someone free, yet still connected to everything. I wished I could move with the freedom of water, and also like the birds that moved above the water. How easy it seemed for them, and for the river, to just be and do, without any thought as to how or why. So why was it so hard for us? I wondered.

It didn't seem to me that life should be as difficult as it was. And I couldn't understand why my thoughts and feelings should remain as they were, confused and without direction. Why couldn't I make a change in myself by making something outside of myself, like the man who had made the rock garden? Every time I viewed his work, I felt a mysterious change come over me. It instilled in me the same sense of wonder that I felt in front of nature. Was there a word for such work? And if there was, who could tell me the word?

Instead of going home, I headed up Erie Street to Hamilton and turned onto La Salle Street until I got to Nicky's home. It was just getting dark, and I was afraid no one was home because the lights in the living room and dining room weren't on. Only the kitchen light was burning at the back of the house when I closed the front door behind me, *Deegen* Roxie appeared in the kitchen door. "Hello, Stepan," she said. "Have you eaten? I'm making *zhkemala monte*."

"No thanks, *Deegen* Roxie," I said. "We ate at five o'clock, as usual. My dad's always starving when he gets home from the factory. Is Nicky here?"

"They've all gone shopping. All but Lily. But they should be home soon, if they don't go to the movies. Do you want to play a record and wait? You love *zhkemala monte*."

"Not as much as Avak," I said.

She laughed and rubbed her hands across her apron before disappearing into the kitchen.

I didn't want to play a record by myself, but I didn't want to go home, either. I could always wait in Nicky's room, I thought to myself as I began climbing the stairs.

The light was shining beneath Lily's closed door. I hesitated and then knocked.

"Come in, Stepan."

"How did you know it was me?" I said as I closed the door behind me.

"By your walk."

"You did?"

"Why don't you sit down."

"I was over at Colbert Park," I said, "and then I came here. Friday nights are sure busy."

"You don't like to shop?"

"I don't like crowds."

"I have the same problem." Lily smiled to show that we were in cahoots.

I smiled back, feeling relaxed. "Do you ever think it's funny that everything in nature seems natural and right and that it isn't something we have to try and understand, whereas whenever man makes something or does something, he puts a label on it if it's something familiar . . . or else . . . well, now I'm confused."

"Were you thinking of something specific?"

"Well, actually I was. The rock garden by Island Park next to the Liberty Street bridge. Does that kind of thing have a name? Well, not a name exactly, a definition, I guess I mean?"

"A number of names," Lily said, and smiled, seeming pleased by what I said.

"It's not what they do that interests me, but why they do it. Because that might explain the effect it has on me."

"They are imitating nature, I suppose."

"Why?"

"Because nature is complete, it's actual, it's already realized. And we aren't, or haven't been yet."

"Haven't been what?"

"Realized—actualized—completed."

"We haven't?"

194

"You're funny," Lily said, smiling again. "But seriously, I'm glad you know that you're troubled about this, because everyone is, but not everyone knows it. That's why people drink, get divorced, have fights, and go to war. These are people who haven't heard that question—inside themselves, I mean. Then there are those who have—more or less—and they get married, hold down jobs, have families, and so on. You're almost too young to ask the question, but I'm glad you have. Just don't be in too big a hurry to find the answer.

"I don't think anyone knows what life is for," I said.

"Wait a minute. Don't talk so fast—and don't talk so big. What you mean is, you don't understand what life is for."

I blushed. She was right. She had found what was troubling me and had given me my question. "How can I know?" I asked.

"By what you do. By what is natural for you. We are part of nature, after all, which means that we *can* know things—certainly those things that come naturally to us. Name some of the things that interest you. Things that you do."

"I like to make lists," I said, which was the first thing that popped into my head.

"Order," Lily said. "What else?"

"I like to draw."

"Form," she said. "And when you were younger, you used to like coloring books, and you were better at it than anyone else. Remember?"

"And what is that?" I asked.

"Proportion, color sense, aesthetics."

"I keep a diary," I said. "It's not just about what I've done that day, but thoughts I've had, descriptions of things I like and want to remember. Stuff like that."

"Understanding," Lily said, "and that's where your question came from—wanting to understand more about life."

"So where does that leave me?"

Lily's smile turned into a laugh this time. "Just where you've always been—but a lot closer to understanding just *where* that is. Be yourself! Don't agree, just to get along; don't disagree, just to be different. Sometimes it's best to speak up; sometimes it's best to keep silent. Do you still run away from home?'

"No," I said, "but I still think about it. How did you know?'

"I saw you once, late at night, at the paperback rack at Ace Grill. I had come out of the Rialto Theater after the last show, and I saw you as I walked by. The streets were all deserted, and there were only two people at the counter—single men drinking coffee. Somehow I knew you'd be going home before long."

"I always went home," I said, "sooner or later. I used to think running away was from being mad at my parents, but I realized now, for the first time, that it's because I'm confused about myself—and angry because of it."

"Are they still giving you a hard time at school?"

"Not so much, not anymore, but I'll never get back those two years they flunked me."

"Don't be so sure."

I felt puzzled again. What did her statement mean? Just then the front door opened and closed. "It's Nicky," Lily said. "He just walked in. Shall we join him?"

Uncle Mihran

"Must you rebel against everything?" my mother shouted. Unlike my father, she rarely lost her temper with me. But I had just put my foot down, telling her I would no longer attend Armenian language classes at the church.

"What good is it?" I asked. "When would I ever use it? Who knows the Armenian language but the Armenians, anyway? We don't even have a country anymore. The Russians own us now, and who cares about them, even, much less us."

196

"That's not why you're not going," she said. "It's because you're ashamed and embarrassed. You think you're too good."

She was right, but I didn't want to admit it. I avoided looking at my father, who was already furious with me, but couldn't think of anything to say that my mother hadn't already said. I looked instead at Uncle Mihran, who was sitting on the opposite end of the sofa from my dad. He looked from me to my mother before speaking. "Let him be," he said. "We think it is hard only for us, but it is also hard for them. Our understanding is imperfect. He has Armenian thoughts that are not his, and are therefore incomprehensible to him, and he has American thoughts that he can't direct because he doesn't know where they come from, either. Let him be confused. What is the harm in that? You can't force him, and if you try it will only make matters worse."

"Let it be worse," my father said. "In that way it can only get better. He will understand when he is grown. Until then he can listen to us."

"Don't talk about me that way," I screamed. "I'm not a dog to be put on a leash."

"He is like you," my mother said to Uncle Mihran, "head-strong, rebellious. Ever since the Armenian church split in two, you have refused both sides."

"I go to the Presbyterian Church," Uncle Mihran said. "There is only one God. In our church God is judged by our fortunes. Since our Massacre at the hands of the Turks He's lost His popularity. After the Massacres politics entered the church, then more grievances, and finally murder. In the church! The Archbishop! Those crazy Tash-naks. The *odars* almost cannot believe what we have done. I almost cannot believe what we have done. I will not forget by going to the *odar* church, but at least the reminder is missing."

I knew what my uncle was talking about. The Tashnaks were a radical political party who insisted on having the flag of the defunct Armenian nation displayed in the church. But Armenia was now a part of Russia, and Etchmiadzin, our Holy See, was also under the sovereignty of Russia. The Tashnaks had murdered the Archbishop in New York, during the church service, for refusing to mount the Armenian flag.

"Let's not discuss it," my father was saying. "What is done cannot be undone. Once the arrow has left the bow, it cannot be called back."

"We cannot fight the Turk, so we fight one another," Uncle Mihran said. "The Turk hates us, and we have come to hate ourselves, and only because their hatred worked, it was effective. What they couldn't kill off they expelled, and now we are like an angry cloud blown across the face of the land. Strangers take us in, but among ourselves we argue and fight."

"What you say is true and not true," my mother said. "We have banded together here, and a new generation has been born. Take a wife and have a child. You will see—there is hope. It is in our children's eyes."

"But from your children's eyes a different world is seen than the one you look at," Uncle Mihran answered. "If they are your hope, what is their hope, hah? Can you know it? Can *they* know it? *Will* they know it if they follow in your footsteps and not their own, hah?"

"What are their footsteps? Show me their footsteps," my father commanded.

I watched as the adults stared at one another in silence. Finally, Uncle Mihran spoke. "Stepan, would you like to come to my church on the corner next Sunday?"

"Sure," I said. "Why not?"

The Black Stockings

"What do you want?" It was my mother again, after me, wanting something—not just for me, but for herself. "Listen to me. Have I

198

told you the story of the black stockings?"

"You've tried," I said. We had been over this so many times before—and I knew without knowing that her story was something more than I could bear. I knew she had suffered, that she had nearly lost her leg and bore a hideous scar from a bomb that had killed two of her relatives and had nearly crippled her. I also knew that she had been orphaned. That we had no relatives, no family photos, no relics from the past. But why would I want to hear about such things? They had happened so long ago, in a place I couldn't even visualize, and concerned an enemy I had never met or even seen, for there were no Turkish families in our town. "I'm not going to listen to you," I said.

"This is not a terrible story. It's not going to hurt you. It hurt me once, a long time ago, but I'm glad it happened because it proved something—to me! When I was a young girl, not much older than you are now, I fell in love with a young man in Piraeus, in Greece, where I later met your father's family. We even went to a movie once after we were engaged. Did you know that? His name was Dickran.

"When it came time for the marriage, my future mother-in-law took me shopping and bought me black stockings because she was in mourning for her husband, who had been murdered by the Turks in Smyrna, where they had always lived. Well, I refused to wear those black stockings, and I backed out of the marriage. You see, she had put her unhappiness ahead of my happiness. Even on my wedding day I was going to be deprived, and not only deprived, but humiliated. That's how it felt to me then. I said no. You see, I had my own mind, I was independent in my thinking, and so that comes from me, how you are. But I was not stubborn, I was not naughty. I knew what I wanted. And I went after it! So what do you want?"

· "I want to be free."

"Tsk!" she exclaimed, pressing her tongue against the roof of her mouth. "That's what I wanted. So I came to America. Would I want something for myself and not want the same for you? This is a free country, isn't it? You are free, aren't you? What kind of talk is this?"

"Safety and freedom are two different things. You earned your safety, I suppose, and I guess I was born in safety—but freedom is something else. And it's different for everyone. Every time I am stopped, it is because I am not free. And everything seems to want to stop me."

"For instance?"

I looked her in the eye, considering what to say, and how to say it. I wanted to say, "Being born," just to silence her, because that was how I felt sometimes.

She was waiting for an answer. "Flunking," I said. "Being flunked because I'm Armenian and don't give a damn about what they have to teach about their great civilization. It'll be great if I'm a part of it. Otherwise the world can blow itself to hell."

"You flunked because you didn't pay attention. Now you have good grades, there will be no more flunking. Your conduct is still bad, but it is also improving. They can't fail you anymore."

"It has nothing to do with conduct or paying attention. They made us change our names, way back in the early grades. That's where the trouble started. I was born Stepan—now I'm Steven. Krikor is Kirk, Haroutoun is Harry. And it began before us, even—Nicky was Nishan—remember?'

"You respect your uncle. He's a wise man. Do you know what he would say?"

"No, I don't know what he would say."

"He would say,' First you must be free on the inside, then the outside won't matter.'"

"Not to him, maybe, but to me it will. When I get to high school, I'll be too told to play after the first year. I'll be ineligible because I'll be too old. I'm the best shot on the basketball team, I'm one of the best fielders on the softball team, and next year I'm taking up football. But after junior high school I'm dead. Why would a coach

200

play a sophomore, if that's his last year of eligibility" I want to be free on the outside. Then I'll be free on the inside."

"That's not how it is. Someday you'll understand."

"Someday! Someday! Well, jam it! I'm leaving!"

"Come back for supper," my mother called after me.

"Maybe I will and maybe I won't." I slammed the door behind me, hoping the glass would shatter. I got on my bike and rode out to the river. I still had the freedom of my bike. I could still be alone. And the river was always there, waiting, in movement, promising change, promising that life could be different because it didn't always have to be the same.

But how could I change my life? Would I have to change myself? Was that the message contained in what she said was my uncle's formula for freedom? Was anyone free? Could anyone be free? And if not, then why could I think of nothing else? If it wasn't attainable, why did I crave it? Was there anything unattainable that you could have even a thought about? Wasn't thinking just as real as anything else? If I thought something, didn't that make it so? Yes, that's right. Yes, yes, I repeated to myself, that's so, but something's missing! What is it, I asked myself. What is it, I asked the river. Tell me! If anyone knows, you do. You know everything about time. It has to do with time, doesn't it? Yes, of course, it's time, isn't it?

No, not time, the river said, but *in* time.

Yes, *in time!* In time, in time, I repeated, again and again as I looked over the water, wanting more of everything than I knew I could have.

I broke a twig and hurled it into the water, and then another and another, and watched them float away downstream, each one a thought, an idea—but none of them an answer.

And then it came to me. I was holding the broken parts of a twig in my two hands. *It has to be accomplished.* Freedom has to be accomplished. It has to be achieved, realized. Yes, that's it: freedom cannot be given, it can only be earned by my own efforts. Did that make it inner freedom? I wondered. Well, it didn't matter how you defined it.

My mother was half right. It wasn't a free country, but free people could live here. Maybe!

The Garden

Uncle Mihran lived in a small house on La Salle Street. He liked sitting on his back porch, which overlooked the garden he had planted with all of the fruit-bearing trees in Wisconsin that he could find. He enjoyed pruning his trees, grafting different varieties for "experimentation," as he said, and doing whatever repairs the trees required. He called his trees "my children," because, he explained, they would always be dependent on him.

I leaned my bike against the porch and joined my uncle "Stepan, it is like this. In the order of *being*, fruit trees are the highest. I am speaking of the tree world now. But fruit trees are delicate, easily hurt, in need of attention and care—tender care—and if abandoned, they soon become wild, food for worms, not for man. Isn't that interesting?"

"Yes, Uncle," I said. I was trying to arrange in my mind all he had told me. "Why don't they teach things like that in school, Uncle?"

"Because in this country they teach from books, and even *about* books, instead of from life and about life. Books instruct, but life teaches."

"What about the good books?" I said. I was thinking of Uncle's books. So far as I knew, he was the only Armenian in town with a library of his own. "Thanks to the Tekeyans, I'm beginning to find books to read."

"That's it, you see—you must find the books that are right for you. In a good school there will be someone to point you in a direction, as the Tekeyans have done in your case. But once you have begun, you must find your own path for yourself—and by yourself. It is no easy matter, but nothing any of us do will ever be more important."

I looked over at Uncle Mihran. He was staring out at his trees, waiting for me speak.

"I don't know what I want," I said. "I only know what I don't want."

"And what is that?"

"I don't want to live in Racine forever. I don't want to be told what to do by people who don't seem to know what they are doing themselves. Which is mostly everybody, especially the old Armenians. Except for you there aren't any adults I can have a serious conversation with. I'd like to speak to the firemen and the blacksmith, and people like that, but they don't seem to want to talk to me."

"They don't have to speak to you for you to learn from them," Uncle Mihran said.

"Why is that?"

"Because if they were to teach you what they know, you probably wouldn't be able to learn."

"Why, Uncle?"

"For one thing, you're not sure what you want. For another, you can't receive instruction the way you are now. You're too angry."

Uncle Mihran turned away to look at his trees again. Two blackbirds were fighting over a plum perched high up in a tree near the garage. "They are coming ripe," Uncle Mihran said. "Everyone wants ripe fruit, but when it is green, eh, then only Uncle Mihran is interested. I care for the green fruit. Everyone else waits for the fruit to ripen. Is that fair?"

"No!"

"No? Are you sure? Life isn't fair, is it? Sometimes, if something suffers over here, something benefits over there, and sometimes these two halves never meet. Maybe they don't even know about each other."

"Do the birds know you are here?"

"Maybe. Maybe not. But the trees know I am here."

"Is that enough?"

"Yes, that's plenty. So what else is bothering you?"

"My mom and dad."

"Yes, of course," Uncle Mihran said, and cupped his chin with his hands. "Just think for a moment. What if you never find your path? What if you find your path and then you lose it, or it is taken from you, hah? How would that be? Your parents love you. Maybe not the way you like, but it's their love, given in their way. You see, our paths have been shattered, but now we have the young ones. You are next. You are our future."

"I've heard that before, and that's just it. I don't want to be their future."

"Then be your own future—*make* your own future. It is the same. It is nothing to be angry about."

"What if I don't know what my future is?"

"You are beginning to know already. That is why you are angry, and also why you fight everyone. But don't begrudge. Don't expect others to understand."

"All right," I said, but I wasn't sure I meant it. I wasn't even sure I understood.

"Good," Uncle Mihran said, and turned to look into his garden again. The sun was beginning to set behind the trees. Several birds were dusting themselves in the rows. I understood now why Uncle kept his garden free of weeds. It was to make a perfect haven for birds. The trees and the garden were as much for them as for the fruit. Uncle sighed, and without turning to look at me, he said, "Just remember, your mother and father love you."

Lily and the Sparrows

I had graduated from Garfield at last and would now be attending Washington Junior High School. I was about to turn fourteen. Now more than ever I wanted to know what the future held for me.

I was sitting on our front porch, sketching sparrows in my new notebook. I had always been intrigued by the family of sparrows that lived inside the towering brick chimney that belonged to the woodwork factory across the street from our house. I was staring at the aperture high up on the chimney that had been made by the removal of one of the bricks. There was one such opening on each side of the chimney. Although they were just ordinary sparrows, their presence in the chimney made them seem magical to me for some reason. It may have been because their homes were visible and yet hidden from view, at a height only they could reach. I wondered now if they weren't reflecting my own life back to me—for I was plain and visible and ordinary, but at the same time I was also secretive and private. But if I was different from others, and separate, it wasn't because I wanted to be or because I tried to be. It was just the way it was. I needed to accept myself—as I was—for that very reason. But it wasn't easy.

I looked up the street and saw Lily walking toward our house. She had taken a job at the J. I. Case office on the corner of State Street and Douglas Avenue, just three blocks away. My mom must have invited her for lunch.

"Making one of your lists?" she asked. "Or are you drawing?"

"I'm not making lists anymore," I said. "I'm trying to describe things with words, but no matter how I try it almost never comes out sounding like my thoughts or feelings. But then every once in a while it *almost* does." I looked up from my notebook, feeling embarrassed and shy. Lily was wearing a kerchief. It was the first time I had seen her with her head covered. The Armenian women all wore funny hats, but their daughters—if they wore anything on their heads—wore kerchiefs. I don't know why it hit me like it did, but in that instant I realized that she would not be going away to music school. It made me wonder if she would stay in Racine for the rest of her life.

She was standing on the sidewalk, trying to decide if she should come in through the front door or go around to the kitchen door on the side, where my mother would be preparing lunch. She said, in a changed tone of voice, "What are you going to do?" I couldn't help but think that she had read my mind.

"I wish I knew," I said. "Tomorrow I go to Washington Junior, but that's not what you mean, is it?"

"No—or rather, yes, that's not what I mean." She laughed and undid the knot under her chin.

"I don't think I want to be an artist, or an architect, or spend all my time in nature as a conservationist, or anything like that. I want to do something that will help me to understand *everything*, and right now I don't understand anything. What good is life if you don't know what it is for?" I stopped speaking and cast my eyes to the sidewalk, feeling self-conscious. But when I looked up at Lily, I saw that she was listening—really listening! I said, "I feel like life is a gift, but that it has to be earned. And I *want* to earn it. Maybe then I will understand what life is for. Do you know what I mean?"

"All too well. You can either feel that way about life, or else you can feel that you are owed. Or maybe that you've been cheated. But neither of those attitudes, or beliefs, will help you to understand, and if that is your aim, well . . ."

"What do you feel?"

"I'm not sure, but I know it is easier to feel cheated or that you are owed. That way you don't have to do anything. And it's hard sometimes not to feel that way. Sooner or later everyone does, if they don't find something to take them away from those thoughts."

"This feeling I have, do you think it comes from me?"

"Does it matter? If you take responsibility for it, then it's yours. That's what matters."

"And if I don't?"

"Then you will lose it. I think that's why some people are bitter. they *become* bitter from not doing what they should do—what *all* humans should do."

"And what is that?"

"You tell me. Or maybe you already have and don't know it."

"How come you know so much, Lily?"

She laughed. "Do I?" She removed her kerchief and shook her hair. After folding her kerchief into a small triangle, she placed it inside her purse. "The more you think about these things, the more you understand—theoretically. But theory isn't interesting, doing is. I know the wrong things. I know what not doing feels like."

I wanted to ask her why she felt that way, but instead I put down my pad in the hope she would continue talking. No adult had ever spoken to me in this way before. With my friends, if I brought up the future, they thought I was crazy. Lily walked up and sat next to me on the porch. I slid over and put my back against the post, so I could look at her face. "I'm ten years older than you, and I was your age when I began to have the kind of thoughts you are having now. You wanted to ask me before why I don't do the things I know to do. I have had to admit to myself that it comes from fear. And also because I consider what others say and think, like my parents, and also the community. Also, I worry. Lots of reasons. I don't think my reasons are very interesting."

I said, "Maybe I'll never find out what I'm good at."

"You have to try. And you have to work at it. It really comes down to effort, doesn't it? We are born with certain possibilities, but we must grow into them through our own efforts and suffering. And if you try, you will see that everything will resist you. Your family, the town, as well as the competition in whatever field you enter. If you can make a force in yourself that is stronger than these obstacles, then their resistance will strengthen you, but if you are weaker than what resists you, then they will weaken you even further. You told me once that none of the arts satisfied you because they each did one thing. Do you still feel this way?"

"Not exactly," I said, and tried to think. "Some writing, especially poetry, isn't so different from music, except that instead of hearing it only with your ear you also feel it inside—but the feeling is similar because poetry really can be musical."

"What else?"

"When I describe something with words, it's not so different from drawing, because I'm just trying to put down what is there. Whether I use words or line and color really doesn't matter."

"I've always thought a well-constructed book isn't so different from a chair or building. . . ."

"Like architecture," I said.

"Yes, like architecture," Lilly said, and smiled.

"I've noticed one other thing about writing. When I write out my problems, I understand them better, because it causes me to line up my thoughts and feelings so I can see them. When I order them in this way, I often see the solution to my problem."

"So maybe writing isn't a compromise for you after all. Also, you can write in private. It can be your secret, and no one need know, because all you need is pencil and paper. Which also means you can travel light." She laughed and started to get up.

Was she telling me that she had tried and then given up? Was that what the look on her face was saying? How had she known that I needed help? She had spoken to me like an adult, and I had understood her like an adult—almost. Maybe I would know better what all of it meant when I grew up. Maybe she was helping me to grow up.

After she had gone inside, I picked up my pad and began sketching again. All at once I felt light inside, and free. I looked up as a sparrow flew straight down from the chimney onto our tiny patch of lawn, which I had recently seeded.

I watched now as the sparrow returned to his chimney home, turning once, twice, before disappearing inside. Someday, I thought to myself, I am going to tell about my sparrows.

Glossary

ahmoht	shameful
basturma	spiced dried beef
choreg	breakfast pastry
Deegen	Mrs.; Madame
jarbeek	enterprising
jeentz	genes
kufta	stuff meatball of ground lamb, onions, nuts, and spices
madagh	sacrifice; as used here, the name of the annual church picnic
odars	foreigners; non-Armenians
peda	Armenian bread
sarma	pigs in the blanket
yavroos	dear one; my dearest
yegour	come here
zhkmela monte	small pasta boats with meat stuffing baked and served in a broth with yogurt